THIS MUM RUNS

Jo Pavey

THIS MUM RUNS

With Sarah Edworthy

YELLOW JERSEY PRESS

LONDON

1 3 5 7 9 10 8 6 4 2

Yellow Jersey Press, an imprint of Vintage
20 Vauxhall Bridge Road
London SW1V 2SA

Yellow Jersey Press is part of the Penguin Random House group of companies
whose addresses can be found at global.penguinrandomhouse.com

Penguin
Random House
UK

First published by Yellow Jersey Press in 2016

penguin.co.uk/vintage

A CIP catalogue record for this book is available from the British Library

ISBN 9780224100427

Typeset in 11/15.9 pt Caslon 540
by Jouve (UK), Milton Keynes
Printed and bound by Clays Ltd, St Ives plc

Penguin Random House is committed to a sustainable future
for our business, our readers and our planet. This book is made
from Forest Stewardship Council® certified paper

MIX
Paper from
responsible sources
FSC
www.fsc.org
FSC® C018179

For Gav, Jacob and Emily

Contents

CHAPTER 1

Back on Track

Come-back races? I've had more than a few, but the night of 10 May 2014 was the ultimate long shot. I was running in the 10,000m National Championships – the 'Night of the 10,000m Personal Bests' – a trial for the European Championships in Zurich that summer. I could look back to pleasing performances in the past and take confidence in being the 2012 European 10,000m silver medallist and a four-time Olympian, but I've always lived in the moment. And right then? I was a forty-year-old mother of two who had given birth eight months before. I trained on a treadmill in a cupboard by the back door and hadn't raced on a track in spikes since London 2012. Was I crazy?

The race was at 9 p.m., which meant it wasn't practical to take the children. So I would have to be away from my baby, Emily, overnight for the first time. It felt like a big deal, an unsettling emotional wrench to leave her and Jacob, who was now a very active four-year-old. I travelled on the train to London the day before the trials so that I wouldn't have to race with 'travel' in my legs, my mind churning through a checklist I'd left for my parents. Mum and Dad were arriving the next morning to look after the kids so that Gavin, my husband and coach, could follow me up to London. I'd be away for thirty-six hours and Gav for less than eighteen, but I wanted babysitting to be easy and fun for my parents and that required a lot of preparation. I stocked up on food, nappies and baby wipes. I rushed around and got the laundry washed and dried. I set out clothes for the kids on the bed in the spare room to save Mum searching through untidy cupboards. I laid out baby sleeping bags and muslin cloths. I wrote a list of roughly when they'd need feeding and with what (fish fingers for Jacob – keep it simple! Formula milk and puréed baby food for Emily). I left notes on other useful information like special tricks we use to get Emily to sleep and made sure they knew how to work the essentials: baby monitor, TV and central heating. I bought nice snacks and real ale for my dad as a little thank-you gift, and made them promise to call me any time, and never worry that I could be preparing for the race. I couldn't be more confident that the kids were in safe hands – just as when Gav's parents help out – but my mind was more at ease knowing Mum and Dad would never hesitate to ring me if necessary. As the train neared London, I imagined what the kids would be doing. Had I remembered everything they might need? My hand reached for my phone. I couldn't resist calling in to get the first update.

Emily was born by Caesarean section in September 2013. Having another little one filled us with so much joy and I didn't want to spoil that very special time with our newborn by worrying about regaining my fitness. I was also determined to breastfeed for as long as possible. I returned to running before Christmas, doing whatever seemed achievable on a day-to-day basis. On my first few runs I had a weird sensation that my legs were not attached to my body; my core muscles would take much longer to recover from abdominal surgery than from a natural birth. I kept breastfeeding right up until April, giving me just a month before the trial to get back to a pre-pregnancy state. Up to that point I was feeding on demand, and Emily resolutely refused to take a bottle of expressed milk, so I couldn't ever be physically far from her. As a result, from the beginning of my journey back to race fitness, all my runs became family runs. Every single one. Sometimes we'd head into the forest – with me or Gav pushing Emily in a running buggy, and Jacob whizzing along gamely on his little bike; sometimes we'd venture into a local park or down the canal path. At track sessions – which involved an hour-long drive to Yeovil because our home track in Exeter was being resurfaced – Gav would coach me, stopwatch in hand, with Emily strapped to his front in a baby carrier, snoozing away, and Jacob sprinting up and down the long jump runway. While breastfeeding, my track sessions were laughable. I ran wearing two or three crop tops to support my lopsided boobs – one emptied from the last feed, the other full in readiness for the next. I had to hope that even though the times I was recording were rubbish, I was still gaining the training benefits. Gav kept reassuring me this was the case: 'Don't worry about the times,' he'd say again and again. In order to boost my mileage and be on hand at home for the kids, I'd pound away on the treadmill we have stashed in a space other people might use as a cloakroom. My children were now my priority, but I couldn't yet contemplate a life without running.

My preparations to 'come back' as an athlete were rushed, guided by every parent's mantra: 'Do the best you can with what you have.' What did I have to lose? I was spurred on by the outside chance that I might represent my country for one more athletics season.

I travelled up from Devon for the 'Night of the 10,000m Personal Bests', hosted by the Highgate Harriers, determined simply to give it a go. I'd normally have entered three or four races as preparation leading up to a National Championships and qualifying trials, but here I was on the night before this very significant 10,000m race, sitting in an anonymous room at the Teddington Travelodge, 150 miles away from my family, contemplating my first race back, a race that was my only chance of qualifying for the 10,000m at the European Championships. I sat there feeling strangely cut off and alone, asking myself all the questions that I have repeatedly been asked ever since I became a mother in 2009: *why* was I still trying to run at an elite level? *Why* was I putting myself through this? To be isolated from our happy-go-lucky domestic chaos felt all wrong, like something was missing in the room. It wasn't until I was chatting to Gav on the phone at about 9.30 p.m., once the kids had gone to bed, that I realised with horror that something much more mundane was missing: my Exeter Harriers vest.

I'd forgotten you need to wear your club vest for national trials. I'd spent hour preparing all the stuff for the kids, and then just chucked my sponsors' kit into my bag on autopilot. It was the sort of thing that would have thrown me into a panic before I had children. Now I was used to taking things as they come with the kids, I just thought how lucky it was that we'd discovered the problem in advance of the event. I told Gav where the Harriers vest was – at the bottom of the laundry basket. (I'm afraid to say it had lingered there because I knew it had to be hand-washed, not just bundled in the machine with everything else.) I said it would need a quick wash and Gav said no problem, he'd bring it up, clean, the following day.

An hour or so later he called again. I could hear in his voice that something was wrong. In the division of domestic chores in our house, there's only one machine Gav's ordinarily allowed near – the coffee maker. And for good reason. He'd only gone and put the vest into the washing machine on a hot wash and it had come out a beautiful Peppa Pig pink. The dye in the burgundy strip across the white had run. It was a complete mess, 'totally unwearable', Gav said – and it was the only one I had.

It was late at night and I started to panic. The rules clearly state you have to wear registered club vests. Racking my brain, I remembered I did have one other – the vest I wore as a junior in the late 1980s, now stashed away as a keepsake in a box of mementos. But where was the box? In the garage? The loft? A cupboard upstairs? Gav was going to have to turn the house upside down to find it and, if he did, I was going to have to run in a vest that was older than most of the girls I was running against.

Quite a while later he rang, triumphantly declaring he'd found the box, eventually, at the back of a wardrobe in a spare room. The vest was inside, he said, but it would need a wash.

'You're having a laugh, aren't you?' I said. 'Just bring it as it is.'

Gav drove up from Devon the following day and met me as I checked out of the Travelodge. He handed over the mothballed vest and we had to giggle.

From 2003 to 2010, Gav and I had lived in Teddington, in south-west London, as so many distance runners do because of the proximity to the running trails in Bushy and Richmond Parks and to Heathrow for travel, so we were back on our old stomping ground. We had lunch in Café Mimmo, a favourite coffee shop, and looked with dismay at the weather outside. It was horrendous, pouring with rain and high winds. As the race was not until 9 p.m., we hoped the wind would die down a bit during the day. But the weather did not abate and we sat in the car for ages, then sheltered in another coffee shop in the park until they turfed us out at closing time. When we arrived at Parliament Hill Athletics Track, we said hello to everyone, then jumped back in the car again to keep dry. Squirming in the passenger seat, I changed into my running kit. I pinned on my number – 41 – and thought they should have given me the number 40.

What were my chances of achieving a qualifying time here? I honestly didn't know. It seemed such a long shot. Having recently stopped breastfeeding Emily, my body was still undergoing physiological and hormonal changes. As an athlete, I understand my body well. I take good care of it; I can read its signals, but I was now primarily a mum who runs and, as any mother who's breastfed knows, your body doesn't quite feel your own immediately post-feeding. How would I perform? It truly was a step – or several thousand strides – into the unknown. I knew that when I put myself on the line, a forty-year-old up against much younger girls, ready to fight it out for medals, I would not modify my approach because of my age. I was aware some of the other athletes had been overseas on winter training camps in preparation; some had run good times in the United States. I'd just been clocking up my miles in lovely Devon with Gav and the kids. I would do what I had always done and simply run as hard as I could. There can be a surprising difference between how I feel when training and how that translates into race form. Sometimes I surprise myself with how much faster I go, other times it can go the other way. The only thing to do was to go into my default mode, give it my absolute all, and see where that would get me.

Despite the dramatically stormy weather, the meeting had a great uplifting party atmosphere. The organiser had been granted permission from England Athletics to allow spectators onto the track to cheer on the runners from lane three. There was live music, real ale and the smell of burgers wafting across the track. Fuller's London Pride sponsored the event, producing commemorative bottles of beer labelled 'Night of the 10,000m PBs' – a nice inspiring touch. The organisers had taken the trouble to ask all athletes for a song in advance to create a playlist for the night; I had chosen U2's 'Vertigo' because I wanted something upbeat with a strong tempo. The rain lashed down; banners and tents strained in the wind. There were some good girls in the field and I had been nervous anticipating the race, but the atrocious weather made us giggle each time we were literally blown off the track while attempting our final warm-up strides – so much so that my nerves evaporated. No one could expect to run well in the blustering gale and that took some of the pressure off. During my warm-up, I had to bow into the wind and throw myself forward to counter the resistance. The wind would let up for a second and I'd have to re-balance or fall over. It was another ridiculous variable which made my mission seem even more unlikely. The comedy of the situation helped me relax.

As I stood on the start line, I pushed all the factors against me doing well out of mind. I thought, 'Let's go for it and see what it brings.' When the starting pistol went, I was taken over by the awesome thrill of being back in a competitive race. Tasha Vernon was the pacemaker for the first few laps, then I decided to go to the front. About midway through, Sophie Duarte of France took the lead for a lap, but I overtook her and pushed on. I was feeling surprisingly okay. It was tough in the gusting wind but everyone was in the same boat and I just felt like cracking on with it. I had to finish in the top two and run under 33 minutes to automatically qualify for the European Championships. Gav had been chatting to fellow coach Alan Storey, the former head of British Athletics Endurance, who thought it would be pretty tough to go under 33 minutes in these conditions, but it was one of those races with no messy moments or sharp elbows or the risk of having your legs cut by another athlete's spikes. After three of the twenty-five laps the race strung out, so I just focused on my rhythm and the track ahead, trying to keep under the qualifying pace as the laps ticked by, my energy boosted by encouraging shouts from the crowd.

I'm never keen on wearing a running vest (as opposed to a crop top) – they look better with baggy shorts, and remind me of PE at school, though I'm not sure why I worry about that when I wear long socks, which is not a good look either – but the decades-old vest proved to be a lucky charm. I knew I was running under the time I needed and I went on to win in 32 minutes and 11 seconds, well within the European Championships qualifying time. I was absolutely delighted, exhausted, soggy, cold, jubilant and relieved all at once. In little over half an hour I had gone from nowhere to National Champion. And I'd won selection to run in the Europeans for my country in my first race back from having a baby! It was bonkers. I congratulated the other girls. Sophie Duarte finished second and Beth Potter had run a brilliant race for third to be the second Brit to guarantee selection. I embraced Gav. We were thrilled but laughing in sheer surprise. Alan shook Gav's hand, shaking his head wryly.

We had an hour or so for the podium ceremony and celebration with friends before the long drive back to Devon. I was summoned onto a sofa for an interview with Tom Bedford, and we had a laugh because Gav thought it was a chat, not a piece of media footage, so he kept barging into shot, at one point opening a beer and taking pictures.

Just after 11 p.m. we set off for home, happy my running career was still on course and our flexible training methods had proved successful. The conversation switched back from athlete/coach to our concerns as parents, juggling children and careers. I couldn't wait to tiptoe in to see our children asleep in their cot and bed, and to read the amusing notes Mum would have written about how things actually materialised despite my original list of ideal food, bath and bed times. I'm not obsessive about routines; we have an understanding with both sets of grandparents that as long as the kids are safe and happy, that's the important thing. It would be amusing to hear how it had panned out.

Chuckling about the vest drama, Gav and I couldn't help but sense how life had come full circle. It seemed so fitting that I came to wear that old vest in the 2014 National Championships because now, at the grand age of forty, I was more than ever like the free-spirited runner who first discovered a love of racing wearing that Harriers vest in the late 1980s. It had been stored away for two and a half decades, a period of time in which many medical experts suggested I give up running and various people tried to modify my approach or make me into a different kind of runner. I continually rebelled (politely) and now – after I had

had kids and moved back to Devon, after I had thrown away piles of orthotic insoles and training gadgets, after my support team had shrunk to just Gav – I had rediscovered my own instinctive, uncomplicated version of running. The experts I had worked with along the way had helped me develop as an athlete. Equipped with that self-knowledge, I had reached a point when I could let my circumstances dictate my training. All I had time to do was to get out there and run . . . My staple run was the five-mile loop I ran as a child; my track sessions were completed at the same Yeovil ground where I'd set a British junior record. It was thrilling to think I'd won my come-back race in the vest that symbolised my innate love of running. Now I had returned to running for pleasure, I was never going to let go of that simple passion. My 2014 season was under way, and little did I know, it would be the mother of all seasons.

CHAPTER 2

The Green Flash Years

My mum, Linda, loves telling people about how as a toddler I never stood still. She says I ran back and forth all the time; there was no stopping me. My parents have this 8mm cine film of me from 1975. The footage is old and fading, but the movement is distinct: it is me, nearly two years old, running up and down pushing a toy cart with great determination. I was too young to be able to recall that day now but my earliest childhood memories are of dashing around. Look at any playground and you see young kids running – milling around, darting backwards and forwards, chasing each other. At that age running is fun, exhilarating, natural. For me, a good thirty-five years on from my playground years, there's still no better feeling than running freely in fresh air, when my body seems weightless, movement effortless, energy is flowing. Pure joy. I fell in love with running right from the off and I haven't lost that passion, even though I'm now also mindful of getting my foot plants right and hitting my target times.

When I was a child, running competitively was not my forte. At the annual primary school sports day we would have the traditional egg-and-spoon and sack races, and a sprint, but the other girls seemed bigger and quicker than me. I never won a race; I never expected to. While I enjoyed it as much as anyone else, I didn't stand out. I had not had the chance to discover distance running, however I loved to challenge myself in my spare time. I used to come home from school for dinner seeing if I could skip non-stop all the way without interruption. I'd find lots of ways to push myself. I loved climbing up to the very top of the fir trees that used to be at the back of the playing fields. I'd sit there, clinging on to the twiggy branches up at the very top, swaying in the wind. On reflection, it was so dangerous! My dad, Bob, was an environmental health officer and my mum went back to work as a maths teacher when I was 12 and later worked as a primary school class teacher. Dad was keen on football and cricket as a boy but had been hindered by poor eyesight in the days before contact lenses became the norm. Mum says that she was always the last girl to be picked to be in a team at school, though at the transport café her family ran in Leicestershire she was always nagging people to play ball games with her in the car park. We laugh because she runs with her arms straight! Physically, though, I can see I have inherited attributes from both my parents. There are certainly no professional athletes in my family history, though Dad's brother, Mike, worked as a PE teacher and ran soccer schools in the United States and wrote a coaching manual. Back in the 1930s, my grandad Alec finished in the top 40 in the national cross-country with very little training. Living in Nottingham with my grandma Stella, he would become my biggest supporter, offering me unusual bits of advice, such as how he used to have a raw egg in some brandy just before a race, and sending me cuttings from athletics magazines with important results underlined in red pen.

I grew up in the pretty village of Feniton in rural East

Devon – about 12 miles or so from Exeter. St Andrew's Church – which dates from the thirteenth century, and where Gav and I were married in 1995 – lies at the heart of the village and the surrounding lanes are lined with high hedges and whitewashed thatched cottages. The nearest town of Ottery St Mary is world famous for its annual tar barrel event on Guy Fawkes Night. The tradition dates from the Gunpowder Plot of 1605 and attracts thousands of visitors each November. It's great theatre and always provides a fun party atmosphere. Every pub supplies a barrel soaked in tar, which is set alight and carried through the streets. Only people from Ottery are entitled to carry a flaming barrel. In the weeks leading up to it, we'd come out of school and see how much higher the town bonfire had been built that day. As teenagers we'd cycle in from Feniton and get stopped by the police on the way home for not having lights on our bikes. We used to wonder how they could reprimand us for that when there were people running around with barrels of flaming tar on their backs.

The town has quite a quirky history, which made it a hilarious subject for comedian Mark Steel's *In Town* programme on BBC Radio 4. He uncovered lots of local eccentricities and had fun undermining our claims to fame. Ottery is also celebrated for being the birthplace of Samuel Taylor Coleridge, so loads of local amenities are named after him despite the poet apparently describing his childhood in Ottery as the most miserable years of his life!

Like most people lucky enough to grow up round here, it was the complete opposite for me – I had a very happy childhood. We lived on an extensive, open-plan estate, built in the 1960s to the west of the original village, so me and my friends Becca, Sarah and Kathryn and all the other kids came together to play. There was a lovely community spirit.

Feniton was a pretty quiet and safe place to grow up, but one of my earliest memories is the Salston air crash. A plane approaching Exeter Airport ran out of fuel and crash-landed right beside the River Otter. Everyone went to see it. My cousins from Derby were staying at the time and we all trekked down to hear the story of the heroic pilot who had managed to land the plane safely away from houses and roads. The only casualties were two sheep.

My two younger brothers, Matt and Jon, and I were out playing or exploring every day. Mum was not one to stay in the house either. She liked to walk in the fields or take the route around the country lanes we call 'the five-mile loop' that I still train on today. The first marker is the lamp-post outside my parents' house, then the route runs out through the village lanes towards Sherwood Farm, up as far as Payhembury, then back by the station, past the shop and back up to the lamp-post. It's hilly but in a good way; tough but doable, and very scenic. The lanes can be caked in cow muck but you can never let that slow you down. When I was young I would use the loop as a marker for my fitness, and I still do so even today. I get nervous about running a good time. Bizarrely, I ran my quickest time on Christmas Day one year. I don't know whether it was due to being fuelled by some strong plunger coffee and lots of chocolate or the fact that Gav, who was following me in the car so that I could see the way with the help of the headlights, had my brother sitting next to him and I had an audience!

But I'm jumping ahead a bit. When I was six, I had an accident that could have threatened my ability as an athlete before I'd even discovered distance running. We had a baby gate positioned a few steps up from the bottom of the stairs to prevent my little brothers from going upstairs. It was normal for me to climb over it when I wanted to get to my bedroom or go to the loo. In those days, baby gates didn't swing open when released; my parents had to take it off its fittings at night and set it back in place in the morning. One day I came downstairs, straddling the gate as usual as I was small and my feet didn't reach the ground, and the gate became unattached. I leant forward to get off it, but the whole thing – including me – crashed into the large window panel at the bottom of the stairs, smashing the glass into daggers. It made such an almighty crash the whole street heard and Mrs Trim, the newspaper lady, abandoned all her papers to run up to the house to see if everyone was alright. I remember the incident so vividly. The first thing I did was shout, 'Sorry, Mum.' I thought only very naughty people broke windows. She rushed to me, anxious to check I was all right, and we both looked down at my left leg. The glass had sliced my thigh from my hip to just above my knee, right down to the bone, leaving the flesh on either side hanging open. My mum grabbed my baby brother and ran across the road to the neighbours who had a car, and in a matter of minutes Mr and Mrs Blackmore were rushing me to hospital with a tea towel stuffed into the gash in my leg. I was lucky not to have severed the femoral artery, which would have meant a very rapid, life-endangering loss of blood. At the hospital, I was stitched up with two layers of stitches because the cut was so deep by our GP, Doctor Ackroyd, dressed in black tie on his way to an evening do. The deeper layer was dissolving stitches; the top layer I had to have taken out at a later stage. I healed quickly, as you do as a child, but I still bear a large scar down my left thigh. Other athletes and physios often ask me about it, assuming I've had surgery as it's so straight, rather than a jagged injury-type scar. The damage has never affected my running, but I think it could have weakened my left leg's basic mechanical capabilities. I would end up having surgery to my left knee, owing to bad tracking of the kneecap (the quadricep muscles in the front of the thigh pull on the kneecap). I would later also have problems with my left Achilles and foot, and have had to battle against the feeling that my left leg is weaker than the right – the sense of it wanting to collapse inwards, which leads to me putting more bio-mechanical stress on my lower leg. However, I was so lucky the injury was not worse, or that I had not gone through the window head first.

Before I discovered running, my first sporting memories are of running after footballs or chasing after my younger brothers in a game of tag. I absolutely loved football and would always be rounding up the kids on the estate for a game in the street, putting out jumpers for goalposts. I would go and watch my brothers play at a local club and I was very jealous that they had the opportunity to play in a team while I, as a girl, could only watch from the sidelines. They were good – Jon won player of the year one season – but my footballing career was restricted to informal kick-abouts, while Matt and Jon got to play proper matches on marked-out pitches with goal nets that would billow out satisfyingly when the ball struck the back. If I hadn't found running, I would have loved to go into football because I adored it. It's great that today there are opportunities for girls to play, and wonderful role models in England's women's football and rugby teams and other sports.

The gaps in age between my brothers and myself are four and six years respectively, so I was very much the big sister, but not a bossy or competitive one, I hope. I've always had a great relationship with my brothers. All three of us loved roller skating and skateboarding – I got my first pair of skates when I was seven, and would spend hours and hours just skating up and down the slope on the road outside our house, often with my friend Lizzie. We used to mark out courses on the pavements with chalk, using different symbols to indicate where we had to do twizzles and so on. We timed ourselves over the course, always trying to beat our previous best. We were lucky to have tennis courts in the village, and I'd spend hours there too with my friends Lynne and Laura. By the time I was twelve, it wasn't uncommon for us to cycle the 13 miles to Sidmouth. My bike was my freedom. I'm very fortunate my parents gave me that scope – though I recall one sunny evening Laura and I were having such a great time on the beach at Sidmouth that we didn't come home on time. It didn't occur to us that our parents would worry. It was such an innocent time. When we finally made it back they were extremely cross, but also extremely relieved.

My brothers preferred skateboarding. That soon became their passion, even more than football, and they worked hard to become skilful. They could do tricks down flights of stairs and jump over dustbins. They made skate videos, and they were serious about practising. I used to watch them work at mastering a trick for hours and hours until they'd nailed it, and admired their single-minded determination.

As siblings, we were a unit, often going to the playing field together to burn off energy. We trusted each other implicitly and were dead against the idea of 'telling tales' on each other. One day Matt and Jon were mucking around on the field when they stumbled over a bin bag full of soft-porn magazines. They were far too young and innocent to understand what they had found. They just thought the images were funny and brought them to show me. Being older I understood a bit more and knew this was not ideal reading material! I was determined not to tell my parents about it. I felt protective of them; the boys trusted me and didn't realise they could get into trouble. So I got rid of the magazines myself. I wasn't always doing them a favour though, a few years later, after I'd started running, my brothers joined the same school and the PE teachers expected them to be decent runners too. When Matt then came last in a cross-country race questions were asked and it turned out that he'd given up on the run halfway round and gone for a swim in the river with his friend Neil! I hope my reputation as a runner didn't make their antics more noticeable . . .

I had nice friends, Laura and Lynne, and a girl called Julia. At primary school, I was moved up a class with another girl who the teachers thought was doing well. Initially it was fun because Becca, my friend from up the road, was in the older children's class, but she moved away to another part of Devon and I suffered from that move. Our parents arranged sleepovers for us and we had lots of fun planning our midnight feasts, but not having Becca at school left me feeling a bit isolated. In the year before I would progress to secondary school in Ottery St Mary, I had to rejoin my rightful year group, and repeat the year. The problem was that everyone had already formed tight friendship groups so it was a bit tough at first – you know what it's like at that age.

It was at my secondary school, the King's School, that I was introduced to the idea of running as a sport. The school had an excellent PE department, and one day my teacher, Mrs Sexty, asked us to run a couple of laps around the sloping grass track of the school sports fields. I took off, went to the front and ran as fast as I could. I can remember as clearly as if it were yesterday. I did my laps and looked back and saw the other kids were still some way from the finish line. Mrs Sexty and the other PE teacher, Mrs Parkin, looked pleased with my performance. Today, there are cross-country clubs at primary school, but in my day it wasn't until we were at senior school and asked to run a winter cross-country or do a couple of laps of a field that natural distance runners stood out. In the playground, you're mostly doing short bursts of running suited to sprinter types. I was surprised when Mrs Sexty took me aside and recommended I join a running club. She'd obviously seen a lot of girls at PE and I was flattered that she thought I showed promise.

The nearest local athletics club was Exeter Harriers, a club that was founded in 1904 and which had 250 or so members across all ages. A neighbour called Caroline offered to take me with her sons, who'd been going along to the Harriers for a while. That in itself was a stroke of luck. When Mum got a teaching job, she arranged for Caroline to be in our house to give my brothers and me a snack when we came home from school and stay until Mum arrived back from work. Caroline suggested she took me to the Harriers' Tuesday- and Thursday-evening training sessions. She and her husband Jim rotated lifts with other neighbours, the Gibbses, whose daughters had also become club members. Living in a rural village without much public transport to rely on could have seriously restricted my development, but I was lucky in that our village seemed to be full of parents willing to spend hours on the endless task of chauffeuring their kids around.

The prospect of walking into a club with such a professional-sounding name was daunting; even travelling into the city of Exeter itself was a fairly major deal. I had butterflies fluttering in my stomach, wondering what I'd be asked to do. Would we be made to run miles and miles? Would everyone be much faster than me? Would I feel out of place? I needn't have worried. It was a lovely, gentle introduction. At first, I was in a group with Ruth Godbeer, and later with a coach called Paul Gregory. They looked after the youngest ones and made sure we had fun through playing lots of games. We'd run around cones and do little relay races; we tried everything – running, jumping, hurdling, throwing events, even piggy-back races. Paul gave us the opportunity to try all the events as well as introducing some longer running sessions. It was a well-balanced and healthy approach to developing young athletes. No one was pressurised to specialise in one discipline too young; it was all about having fun.

When I was about thirteen, Paul and another coach, Martine, took us all on a training camp to Swansea, which was great fun, and a real eye-opener for me. All the other kids said they couldn't go training during a particular part of the day because they had to watch *Neighbours*. The Australian soap had just started being shown in the UK and was so popular. I'd never seen it before but came to love it too. Many years later I would win a road race in Melbourne, where the programme is filmed, and was awarded my trophy by the member of the cast who played Ruth. She told us that her character's wedding to Phil was due to be filmed in a few days' time so we could go along to meet the cast. We did – and I even took a novelty photo of me pretending to train on Ramsay Street.

I soon settled in at the Harriers and when it became clear that distance running was where my natural talent lay, I moved to the endurance running group coached by Tony White. He suggested initially I trained one night a week with Paul and another evening with him to make the transition easier. I was fourteen when I moved to Tony full time and was excited to be in the same group as Emma Sokell, Cathy Hulme and Liz Taylor – these girls were the stars of the club and I aspired to be like them.

Tony ran his squad on a handicap basis so the slowest set off first on a session and the quickest went last. Even so, I started leaving some of the boys behind. Tony likes to recall how he asked them if they were just being gallant in letting me always come in first, and one of boys replied in exasperation: 'Far from it! I can't go any bloody faster!'

Soon, I was running with the older boys, and eventually with the men in the group, getting faster and stronger by the week. It was a great time. When I first joined the club I used to get through huge numbers of Green Flash plimsolls, touched up regularly with loads of shoe whitener. I'd run until holes appeared. I was never happy unless I was out in front, even in a training session, and each time I moved up a group, I wanted to prove myself. I was challenging myself just as I had when I used to try to skip all the way home from school for dinner. Tony's handicap system for a track session was a double challenge – not only to run an impressive time according to the target he set, but also to do the mental maths it required. He set us individual time slots. He would set the slowest at, say, 18.5 seconds per 100 metres, the middle range runners 17.25 – yes, he even did quarters of seconds – and the fastest at 16, and then he'd count down to the start and you had to work out when to go so that we all finished together on the line. The time set would vary according to the session. Then you had to take the average, adapt your time to real time, and tell him how well you'd done. I found this quite acceptable, but I now realise how unique it was. No wonder maths became my best subject at school.

Running gave me a sense of identity, of achievement and purpose. I loved the spirit at the Harriers, both the running and the social aspect, and I became determined to improve. Prior to joining Tony's group, I used to go running every day at school at lunchtime, in the winter doing the road loop around Ottery St Mary (trying to do it in 13 minutes) and in the summer escaping down to the grass track to do an 800m. I had no concept of how you structure training, of breaking a certain distance down and doing repetitions instead of just running the whole length. I used to go for runs before school, too. That shocks me now: it shows my motivation because I'm not a morning person at all. On dark mornings or evenings, Mum would follow me in the car so that I could see courtesy of the headlights or Dad would accompany me on his bike. Another neighbour, John Kimbrey, a former Royal Marine who was the father of my brother's best friend, also used to take me on long runs on the roads around home. These outings stretched me. John was a training instructor at the Royal Marine Commando training centre at Lympstone and we worked off each other. He gave me lots of encouragement and I think he liked to taunt his Marines that he went running with a young girl who could keep up with him!

As far as my parents were concerned, running at Exeter Harriers was my hobby, just as the boys had their skateboarding and surfing. I loved the Harriers. The club was full of characters and selfless volunteers. If it hadn't been for the coaches, the people making tea, the supportive parents, no one would have had a chance to take running seriously. It was thanks to a community effort that I was able to consistently show up to the training sessions and stick to the schedule Tony set. I've always been grateful to Caroline and Jim and to the Gibbs family for the lifts. All three of us had our own interests and places we wanted to be. Dad did a hell of a lot of long-distance weekend driving, taking my brothers on day trips surfing in Cornwall or getting me to Solihull, Stoke or Crystal Palace for competitions. They cheered us on, but let us get on with our hobbies ourselves. We rarely had our picture taken on our own; my parents liked to take photos of all three of us together. They didn't like to single one out. When we were together it was family time and we didn't talk much about each other's individual pursuits. They didn't make a fuss about any of our personal successes because they were mindful of the other two and thought it's not a mark of a person how well they pass an exam or do in a sports event.

Mum thinks it's comical, looking back on it now, how little they knew about running in those days. If people asked about my training regime, they hadn't a clue. It wasn't until another parent offered us her daughter's old pair of spikes for £5 that I had my first pair. Up until then I ran on the track in my Green Flash plimsolls. 'Poor child! We were terribly ignorant,' Mum says, but it was such an innocent period. I ran with so much joy and enthusiasm and I consider myself very lucky with the support I had. My parents didn't become overly involved or monitor my progress or discuss the ins and outs of my performances. As a result they never put pressure on me. I was quite good enough at doing that to myself. Their lack of knowledge about running meant they couldn't be pushy parents if they tried. And we did see some! Mum and I once witnessed a father shouting angrily at his daughter, saying he wouldn't give her a lift home – all because she hadn't beaten me. That was how this particular parent often behaved. His face would turn bright red; he looked like he was about to explode. He was a good example of how not to parent a young athlete. Another time, I was stretchered off after collapsing on the track, and Mum ran down anxiously asking if I was all right. 'Of course she's not,' growled another parent. 'She should have won the race.'

It's incredible how pushy some parents are. Mine appreciated seeing how running had quietly given me a passion, but it was my interest, not theirs. They didn't interfere at all. Mum used to accompany the girls' cross-country team on the coach. There weren't shelters at these events so she was known as 'the bag lady': Tony asked her to look after all the girls' bags while we raced to give her a role. Mum and Dad were proud of my progress but they weren't living out their own fantasies through me; they never asked me to prioritise homework over running, or vice versa. They simply wanted me to do what I enjoyed and didn't see how hard I was pushing myself. I enjoyed working towards goals. It was as simple as that. I've always taken life as it comes and got on with it. I knew I needed to do my homework, so I did it. I knew I needed to run, and to get better at running, so I did the work Tony set for me. But I did feel extremely tired a lot of the time. I gave up piano lessons because it was too much on top of tennis and netball at school as well. Every day, going into training or weekend competitions, I put pressure on myself. But I hid it well.

CHAPTER 3

1988 – Surprise Success

By the age of fourteen I had moved full time to Tony White's endurance running group. Tony has been an amazing supporter throughout my career – and he still is, even though he is long retired and lost his sight more than twenty years ago. He is an incredible person, a truly selfless man, as shown by all the hours he gave as a coach. When his wife sadly became ill, Tony was her devoted carer even though he himself was blind by then. He still walks several miles a day with his guide dog and he still goes up to the club twice a week with an assistant who is his 'eyes'. Back in 1987, Tony saw something in me – 'Little Jo' as he called me, because there was a taller Jo in the club. He was a hard taskmaster – all coaches are – and what I always needed was someone to rein me in and hold me back, but he was also like a family member. Our bond was immediate even though he likes to tease me about the number of times he would affectionately call me a little madam for defying his race tactics in order to run at the front, or to run at all when he thought I was risking injury. I suppose I always enjoyed the thrill of trying to run fast.

In the winter of my first year under his guidance, we did a lot of cross-county and road races, a 'means to an end' to strengthen you up for the summer track season, Tony explained. On Tuesdays I would go out with the older boys on a road run. Tony gave us high-visibility bibs and he and his assistant Les followed, either in his three-wheeled Reliant Robin or in Les's beige car. They'd suddenly appear at mile markers, jump out of the car and shout times at us. As one of the faster ones, I'd be held back before starting a road run because the idea was that we'd all finish together – which we never actually did – and so I missed Tony or Les calling out my times after the first few miles.

On Thursdays he set us a track session at Clifton Hill in Exeter. I have so many good memories of those evenings under floodlights. Way back then, before the wonderful Exeter Arena was built in 1992, we had no synthetic all-weather Tartan tracks in deepest darkest Devon. Unlike most of my rivals outside of Exeter, I trained on a cinder track, a concrete surface covered with a light dusting of cinders – not the best surface for young kids to be training on, really, as it's so hard. Running on the tail of a pack of men meant I'd finish with grit and mud splashes on my face and down my front; but running for so long on a cinder track would prove an advantage, too. The first time I ran on a Tartan track it was so much easier, so much lighter, I felt like I was flying. The Clifton Hill sports centre was next to a dry ski slope, and we'd be slogging around the track only to look up and see people nonchalantly skiing down a gentle slope next door. The clubhouse was a jumble of chairs and tables, illuminated by flickering fluorescent strip lights. There were some weights in the corner and a kiosk in which two lovely ladies served crisps, chocolate and tea or coffee in white polystyrene cups. I never saw my pace in the context of other runners, or compared my times; I simply loved to run. At weekends Tony suggested I do a good thirty-minute evening run around my local playing fields on the grass to save my legs. The fields in Feniton were small so I had to keep going past the cricket clubhouse, which I found very embarrassing. The cricket team would be in the bar long after their match was over, and the groundsman would be on his tractor, and I'd feel self-conscious about running round and round by myself.

1988 was a crucial year for me. In the space of a few years I had gone from someone who didn't know I had a talent for running to being a fully committed member of an athletics club with a race schedule. In those early races, I clearly remember the exhilaration of getting to the front, trying to go faster and faster, carefully gauging my pace according to Tony's advice. Within weeks I had developed an absolute love of track racing. I adored that feeling of running at the front, being chased down. It was such a thrill, almost animal-like, running scared, excited, trying to keep ahead of the chasing pack, hoping no one would catch me before the line. One day Tony asked me to get my mum or dad to come and see him after training the following Thursday.

'Why? What's wrong?' I asked.

'Nothing,' he said, without further explanation.

It turned out he had decided to put me in for the Southern Counties Championship at the New River Stadium in Haringey. He told Dad he thought I might 'cause a bit of a surprise'. So Dad drove me to north London for my first championship Junior Girls 1,500m race. I was pretty silent on the journey, terrified. Tony said there were four very strong girls in the field and he thought I'd get extended. 'This is not going to be easy, okay?' he said. I was daunted by the prospect of racing at all. In fact, I was so nervous I vomited before the start.

The gun went. Ignoring Tony's tactics, I ran to the front and carried on pushing to the finish line. I won with a time that was only half a second outside a record that had been held for twenty years.

To my continuing surprise, I won all my races in the lead-up to the big ones that year: the English Schools Championship and the AAA (Amateur Athletic Association) National Championships. I was nervous for the English Schools, but equally I couldn't wait. My simple approach of running to the front, enjoying the thrill of the chase, trying to get faster, was all I knew. Although I cared about the end result, it was the excitement of the race itself I was becoming hooked on. The English Schools was staged that year at Yeovil, on the very same track I ended up training on in 2014 when my home track at Exeter was closed for resurfacing. The tradition was for each school athlete to stay with a host family. Though they were lovely, welcoming families, it ramped up the level of nervous discomfort. You'd be a shy teenager doing the championship of your life and staying with people you'd never met before, sitting at dinner making small talk, staying in someone's spare bedroom. Today the English Schools competitors stay in youth hostels because of child protection laws.

On the day, I was consumed by nerves, but not sick as I'd been before the Southern Counties. I just went to the loo about forty times. It felt like I imagined an Olympics would, but I was probably more nervous than I would be later on for the Olympic Games. This meeting felt so massively important. When I see youngsters competing now, I know what great experiences and memories they are gaining, though I also feel empathy with them because I know all too well the pressure you put on yourself at that age. The pressure can be worse because you haven't learnt how to cope with it or understand that nerves manifest themselves in different ways. At fourteen or fifteen you feel so grown up, but you have no idea how narrow your perspective is. At a championship I felt very heavily the pressure of performance, of expectation, of not wanting to let down my club, my teammates or Tony. My dad says now that he could tell, driving me to races, how nervous I was and how I tried hard to hide it. In my earliest races I remember the nerves, but also the thrill of trying to be competitive and working to put in the best performance I could. That's a sense that's stayed with me through my career.

These memories are balanced with the great times I had as a member of the Exeter Harriers team: travelling on the coach with my friends, cheering each other on in our events, bellowing at the side of the track, stopping at the motorway services to buy sweets on the way home. We were all competing to get valuable points for the team. We often had to do a random event for points – you'd get one point even if you came last. These points would be crucial to boost our club's position in the league. I'd often find myself doing hurdles or long jump. We'd have a laugh as there was no pressure. The fun camaraderie of being part of a team was definitely a factor that kept me interested in athletics for so long.

Before the English Schools 1,500m final, we had to sit in the 'call room' before our race, following the routine of a senior meeting, with the atmosphere growing increasingly tense. The call room is where the stewards check your bib numbers and make sure everyone is dressed according to the regulations. It's a strange atmosphere because you sit surrounded by all your track rivals. Some people sit quietly while others move around and stretch nervously. I remember the relief of finally lining up to start. It was a damp and windy day, but that hadn't deterred all my family from coming to support me or the crowd from cheering every race vociferously. I still have a video of the race and those few minutes of film capture my entire 1988 season: me in my Devon Schools vest and distinctly 1980s running knickers, Tony with his stopwatch positioned at the 200m point – his preferred perch – so he could see directly across the field to time me by the lap as well. The gun went off and I moved to the front, and enjoyed the buzz of trying to run faster and faster with each lap. I could hear my club mates urging me on. Tony had warned me that Heidi Hosking from Cornwall was my biggest threat and she hung on my coat-tails. We left the rest of the field behind over three laps. From his trackside position, I heard Tony call, 'Jo, you've got to go . . .' and I duly sprinted down the back straight – 'like a scalded cat', as he describes it – with Heidi now 10 metres behind. I crossed the line; I'd done it. The official result read: Joanne Davis, 4:27.9. Not only had I won, I'd set a new British Under-15 record.

The previous record stood at 4:31, and Heidi went under it too. I was genuinely shocked, and excited, but could not take it in. At the finish line I saw Tony and Mrs Sexty, who had supported me from my very first attempt at distance running. It's still an amazing memory. Tony's faith in me was validated, and he still talks about being chuffed to find himself being congratulated by Linford Christie's coach that day! There was a chill on the breeze. I recall feeling a bit hypothermic and my gran had to be taken back to the car because she was frozen. It seemed surreal – what did it mean to be an English Schools Junior 1,500m Champion? If you look through the record books you see that few juniors stay the course to become senior athletes. But also in the field of the 1,500m that day in Yeovil was Paula Radcliffe from Bedfordshire. We later became GB teammates, of course – and she went on to have a stellar career. We were two fourteen-year-olds among a hundred other juniors from different parts of the country competing in our biggest race yet. Both being from the West Country, Heidi and I became friends and I went to stay at her house in Cornwall to train with her. She took me for a session on the sand dunes near her home and completely thrashed me. Horses for courses, as they say.

It is funny when I look back on the English Schools now and see so many seeds of my future life: Tony steering my running career, me loving the thrill of the race, and Gav, my future husband, in the crowd watching. He remembers seeing me run as a fourteen-year-old and it's magical to us that he was there that day, although we didn't meet each other until the following year, in 1989, when he joined Tony's group in Exeter. In 2014 we went training as a family to the same Yeovil track, and we have a funny photo of me passing the finish line with Emily sitting on a rug on the grass right next to it. We can contrast this new photo with one of me at the same point in the race in 1988.

Back at school, the PE staff kindly wanted to award me my medal in school assembly. Rather than feeling proud, I dreaded the moment my name would be called out and I'd have to walk up to the front past hundreds of boys and girls to receive my prize. My dedication to running – disappearing off at lunchtime to run, having a talent for something – had sometimes made me a target for bullies. Times have changed and now youngsters are celebrated for their individual interests and achievements, but some girls made a point of being unkind to me because of my commitment to running. None of the girls in my form were interested in sport so I stuck out from the crowd at that very age when teens tend to hang out in packs, but I think fondly of the King's School and of the lifelong good friends I made there, like Caroline, and especially Mrs Sexty, who was key to my running career. Today I feel very honoured to know my running vests hang on the wall there.

School broke up for the summer holidays, but I was still working on my running dreams. Next up was the AAA National Championships at the Alexander Stadium in Birmingham, a meeting which for the first time also incorporated the GB trials for the 1988 Seoul Olympic Games. I was very fortunate because that was the year it was decided to hold the U15 races there, too, for youngsters to gain experience. The Olympic trials are always a huge deal. In 1988 crowds flocked to Birmingham to see the likes of Steve Cram, Sally Gunnell and Colin Jackson. To qualify, each athlete needs to have run an 'A' standard time, and to finish first or second in the trial. And there's a third, discretionary spot, too. There is a lot of potential drama. Fans would camp overnight in the nearby parks and join the very long queues for tickets to gain entry. As a fourteen-year-old, it was incredible to compete in that feverish atmosphere. My journey there was suitably epic, too. As Dad was down in Cornwall with his brother Mike, who was on a rare visit over from the States, my mum and I travelled up to Birmingham on the train. We took a bus to the hotel, and then found another bus to get us to and from the stadium each day where we met up with my teammate Liz Taylor and her parents.

The meet took place over three days, which left me scope to race in both the 800m and 1,500m. On Friday it was the 800m heats; on Saturday the 800m final and on Sunday the 1,500m, which was a straight final. The temperature was searing on Saturday and by the afternoon you could have fried a full English breakfast on the track. You could feel the heat radiating off the running surface. The whole scene blew my mind. Compared to the English Schools Championships, staged down the road from me in Yeovil, the AAAs seemed like it was on the scale of an Olympics. Everything felt bigger, louder, brighter: the noise of the crowd and the stadium announcements, the scale of the timing technology and scoreboards, the different areas to warm up, warm down. I felt extremely nervous and under pressure, with the expectation on me following the English Schools result.

I considered the 1,500m my specialty, but first up was the 800m. Tactically I raced my heat as I always did, front-running all the way. I approached the final the following day in the same spirit. Two Irish girls stuck to me, but I surged and managed to break away from them to win in a personal best of 2:12. As I crossed the line, I didn't have time to register an emotional response to my win. My feet were absolutely killing me. They were so painful I sat down as soon as I could. I couldn't face warming down. I told Tony and we both looked down at my feet. Blood was slowly seeping out of my spikes. I thought it must be blood blisters. He suggested my mum take off my spikes and socks. Horrified, she tried to take off one very cautiously but blood started gushing out, and my socks seemed stuck to my feet. Mum managed to ease the spikes off my other foot too and the first-aiders took over. I had to have the socks soaked off from both feet. The heat from the track had scorched the skin, and it tore off, leaving the surface of both soles red raw. It was a terrible sight. Tony had never seen anything like it.

'How on earth did you finish the race with pain like that?' he asked.

I thought back to the last lap. I was in a bit of pain, it was true, but I knew it would be over in seconds, so I put my head down.

The first-aiders cleaned my feet and told me to keep off them for a few days to allow them time to heal. They said I must not run. Mum went off to find a chemist for blister packs and came back with sanitary towels, too, to cushion my feet and mop up the blood that was still flowing. The drama over, I looked back on the 800m final and tried to enjoy the fact I'd won. But the 800m wasn't the reason I was there.

'Jo, my love, you're not doing the 1,500m tomorrow,' Tony said gently.

'Don't worry, Tony, I'll be fine.'

'Jo love, you can't. Your feet are in no fit state.'

'Don't worry, Tony; they'll be fine tomorrow.'

We left it at that. In the evening we had a pub dinner with the Taylors, and then went back to their family caravan. I sat in the front seat, banked up on cushions with my feet dangling out of the window, enjoying the cooling sensation of a light breeze on my burnt feet. The first-aiders had told me to make sure my feet got plenty of air. After a while Tony came over and said he and Mum thought I'd exposed my feet long enough now, and I should put on the blister packs to prevent infection. I did that . . . and put my trainers on. To Tony's horror, I went off to have a little jog. I hadn't warmed down and I wanted to do the best I could to prepare for the 1,500m final. Everyone had told me not to run, but nothing they said was going to change my mind. A little bit of pain wasn't going to stop me. Why wouldn't I still want to run?

The 1,500m final was at 3 p.m. the following day, and it was, I had to admit, pretty hot again. Clocking my determination to race, Tony said he needed to see me run in my trainers to check I was fit. I warmed up under his beady eye and he didn't detect any limping whatsoever. I was honest when he asked me how I felt. I did feel a bit sore, as I suspected I would, but it wasn't anything I couldn't overcome. I knew I'd be able to hold it together over 1,500m. I had already decided I wasn't going to put my spikes on until just before I lined up. I warmed up and did my pre-race strides in my trainers – and as he took me down to the start line Tony made me promise I'd stop if I felt uncomfortable. Then he went off to watch, muttering 'Little madam' under his breath!

There were twelve girls in the final. The gun went. I moved to the front as usual, put in a steady first couple of laps, not putting undue pressure on my feet, then took off halfway down the back straight, running away from the field. The bell was my signal to accelerate as much as I could on the final lap and it was a fantastic feeling, stretching my legs and putting every ounce of energy into crossing the line first. I'd won again! I waited to shake hands with all my competitors as they crossed the line, and then went over to debrief with Tony.

My feet were killing me, but I didn't care. I was so excited about another win. Mum nervously removed my spikes and socks again, and there was less blood this time. I had run with my feet wrapped in sanitary towels.

The summer of 1988 was a turning point in my life. At the AAAs I became the first U15 ever to do the double – win both the 800m and the 1,500m. And I'd set a new U15 national record for the 1,500m. In running I'd found something I absolutely loved and something I wanted to pursue with single-minded determination. Tony likes to say that the day of the 1,500m final was the day he learnt what sort of a person and an athlete my fourteen-year-old self was – and the extent of my pain threshold! He could see in my unflinching determination exactly what running meant to me.

People came up to me that weekend and kindly said I had a bright future ahead of me. I couldn't see it though. It was satisfying to achieve the goals I'd set but I never had a high opinion of my abilities. In that first ever combined AAAs National Championships and Olympic Trials, I had watched the same seniors race that I'd seen on TV, raced the junior events alongside them, and thought, 'How on earth can they run like that?' I couldn't see a trajectory stretching from a junior athlete into senior competition. My GB Junior record for the 1,500m was 4:27. How was it humanly possible to run that distance sub four minutes – almost half a minute faster – when my experience over that distance already was of pushing my body to a point where there was nothing left inside me. I didn't leave Birmingham thinking, 'That's it, I'm going to become an Olympic athlete.' All I knew was that I enjoyed running and the lifestyle it gave me. I loved going to the club and going away to compete at weekends. I loved trying to better my PB. I loved leading a race . . .

My instinct to front-run my races was going to be a hard one to relinquish. What that summer of 1988 had taught me was that unless I was out in front I wasn't happy. In 1989 Tony asked me to experiment a bit with the 800m; he wanted me to work on different race tactics and speed and to become more race-savvy. He set me a target of achieving an 800m personal best, which happily I did. However, after my surprising successes of 1988, the following year was up and down. I had the highlight of being picked by the GB selectors for the Under-20 team and ran in Athens. I was excited to be chosen to represent my country in a junior international competition, and to travel abroad and compete in the huge stadium with athletes I looked up to like Donna Fraser. We were taken to visit the marble-stepped Panathenaic Stadium. Seeing that black hairpin-shaped track, built on the remains of an ancient Greek stadium, was fascinating.

But as a whole, 1989 was a disappointing year. I struggled with injuries – shin splints, Achilles problems. Youngsters develop and have growth spurts at different stages and my body was changing. I lost some of my energy, and I couldn't understand it. I was training harder and running slower. It seemed the reverse of what should be happening: shouldn't I be getting faster as I grew older and stronger and trained harder? It's a phase you often see in girls. Going through puberty can take a lot of your energy for a while. I wish I'd understood that at the time. I just couldn't comprehend why I wasn't improving and I grew very frustrated with myself. I make a point of explaining this when talking to young athletes now: everyone develops at different stages.

Nonetheless, no injury was going to take my joy in running away from me. Over the years I would develop a bit of a reputation for being 'stubborn' – but only in a running context, I hope! I prefer to think of myself as determined. To this day, I have such a passion for running and racing that I never want to be told to stop . . .

CHAPTER 4

Gavin

Gavin Pavey, a keen 800m and 1,500m runner himself, was also at the AAAs as a spectator and supporter of Devon's athletes. When we look back at that day in Birmingham now, I recall my races, the people I met and the famous athletes I got to see perform, while Gav remembers thinking, 'Oh, there's that girl from Exeter again . . .' We hadn't met when he approached Tony White and asked if he could join the Harriers.

Gav is two years older than me, so when he first joined Tony's group in the late summer of 1989, I was 15 and he was 17. On his first evening training with us – so the first time I met Gav – Tony set him off on a five-miler with me. And he couldn't keep up! He was gasping for breath, but determined to stay with me for his ego's sake. After a while he had to drop back. I was this little kid in blue Lycra tights, and I left him for dead. Quite an amusing way to meet your future wife! We got on from the very beginning though. He was supportive rather than competitive. Many other teenage boys might have taken a bit more of a blow to the ego at being beaten by a girl two years their junior – though he soon found his form once he'd got some sessions under his belt. I liked him as a friend, but as time went on it became clear that he wanted to be a bit more than that. He was a bit of a stalker – as he puts it himself – phoning me at home every night – any excuse – and we'd talk for hours. His excuses to call became more and more ridiculous, which amused me. He'd ring to ask if I had somebody's phone number, which I knew he didn't need, then the next night he'd ring again saying he'd lost it, and needed it again. I didn't fall for any of it. He'd come and hang out at Exeter College – where I'd moved for my A levels – even though his college was 20-odd miles away. At the time I was going out with a boy at my college and I had no intention of 'being unfaithful' to a good guy, so even though I liked Gav I refused to call him back.

My time at Exeter College was extremely happy. We had our little posse – Rachel, Rupert, another Rachel, Sophie and Paul. My close friend Rachel Staddon also ran at Exeter Harriers, and Rupert often went running with me at lunchtimes. I loved my new-found independence and the grown-up feel that the sixth-form college gave me. When my relationship with my boyfriend ended, my first instinct was to pick up the phone and call Gav. He took my call out of the blue as a signal that our 'just friends' status might be about to change. As I was just seventeen, Gav decided it was proper to ask Tony if he could ask me out on a date. So, apparently, one night after training Gav sidled over to Tony and asked for a quiet word.

'I don't know how to put this,' he said nervously, 'but how would you feel if I asked Jo out on a date?'

'I wouldn't feel any different!' Tony said. 'It's up to Jo to decide if she wants to go on a date with you . . .'

Tony later said he was quite chuffed. Gav asked me out properly and we went on our first date on 24 October 1990. We headed into the bright lights of Exeter and had a great time. It was typical teenage fun, packing in as many activities in a day that we could normally only afford in a month. We went to the cinema to see *Presumed Innocent* – it was just what was on – followed by bowling, and ended up in SpuduLike. Up until then, we'd mostly bonded through the Harriers, but the dynamic in our relationship changed straightaway, and we fell deeply in love. We started doing everything together, from going out with mates to volunteering for sports days for the disabled. We bonded over music too, both being big U2 fans. It became our routine to meet for dinner every Tuesday and Thursday evening before going up to the club to run in Tony's group. We would go to the Boston Tea Party and order Boston grill with chips and, as if that wasn't enough fuel, we'd follow it up with a trip across the road to buy Mars Bars. It is hard to believe now, but we genuinely thought this was good preparation for a session. We both often suffered with gut problems during training but strangely never attributed it to our pre-session meals.

Soon it was time to invite Gav to 'meet the parents'. They already knew him a bit from seeing him at a few races, but he'd never been to my house. On his first visit to the Davis household he was obviously keen to make an impression – but not the impression he ended up making or should I say 'leaving' throughout the house. We'd been for a run together first, then come back home. After getting a drink from the kitchen, we wandered through to sit in the lounge. My mum came in but before she could greet Gav, she wrinkled her nose in revulsion and exclaimed, 'Oooh, what's that smell?' A bit of further sniffing revealed the awful truth: Gav had trodden in dog muck and brought it in on the bottom of his trainers, leaving marks all through the hallway and into the lounge. . .

After the dog muck incident, Gav obviously felt he needed to get my family on side, and we were all amused by the lengths to which he went to impress my brothers. He used to ride BMX bikes so, eager to prove he was cool, he would cycle over and show off in front of my parents' house. His main trick was a somersault over the handlebars – a trick he occasionally still does in our garden today, to impress our son Jacob, ever the kid at heart. After all the phone calls, the dog-poo episode and the BMX showboating, Lord knows what my parents thought, but Mum says she knew Gav was 'the right one' when she came home to find a note from him pinned on the fridge. 'Don't worry,' he'd written. 'Jo's in hospital. I've packed her a bag and that's where we are now.' The day before I'd had an accident in the chemistry lab during my mock A level practical exam. The task was to identify an unnamed chemical. I had undertaken a series of basic tests, but had seen no initial reaction from my mystery substance, so I'd pushed my protective goggles back on my head. Without warning, there was an explosion in my beaker and the chemical – which turned out to be hot sodium hydroxide, a strong alkali also known as caustic soda – bubbled up like a geyser into my eye. It was agony, and the teacher told me I should get my mum to take me to the eye hospital. Mum found me sitting on the pavement outside college and took me straight to the eye specialist. I was treated and came home, but overnight the pain was still unbearable so Gav decided to take me back in the next day when everyone else was out. The alkali solution had burnt off my cornea and I ended up staying in isolation in hospital for a week to avoid infection while the cornea grew back.

Thankfully when I met Gav's parents and his brother, Alex, and sisters Julie and Alison there were no such mishaps or drama. They were very welcoming to me; Alex even gave me his treasured horseshoe from one of their grandad's favourite racehorses as a good-luck memento.

It's funny to look back at how young and naive we were and think that the eighteen-year-old boy who we joked about stalking me is now my husband, my coach, my physio, my race manager, my best friend and the father of my children. I don't know where I'd be without him. We finish each other's sentences, guess what the other one is thinking, say the same thing at the same time – although I'm sometimes left thinking, 'Did he really say that?!' He has always been able to make me laugh. If something goes wrong, his default is to find humour in a situation and that is a priceless quality. Since first meeting we've gone through life together in a happy-go-lucky way and never consciously worked on planning for the future. Life just unfolded in front of us. When Gav went to university in Bristol ahead of me and I eventually followed him, we always knew we would live together. As students, we even put our money together in a joint account. I regard it as luck. I met absolutely the right person for me at a ridiculously young age. We all have our 'what if' moments that map out our lives. It's extraordinary to think that if one element of our early story had been different – if Gav had not wanted to join Exeter Harriers or something – then it wouldn't have been.

CHAPTER 5

The Lost Years

As a runner, you often do 'interval sessions' – short periods of hard effort where you run fast, with recovery periods in between. When children play they often do lots of short bursts, a bit like an interval session, but the difference is they aren't doing it for anything other than for fun. Their natural instinct is to move fast. They'll stop and start again constantly, like when they are dashing around playing tag. As soon as they can walk, they want to run. Saying 'I'm going out for a run' sounds a perfectly valid, sensible activity to a child. Running? It's simple. They get it. However, I would struggle to tell my children that running is my job. I've never viewed it that way myself; I just feel so lucky to be doing something I love and to share my passion for running with Jacob and Emily. They are so used to me running; they wouldn't think to question it, especially as we regularly go training as a family outing – unless I'm running on the treadmill. Sometimes I wonder whether athletes are people who never lost that simple love of running, who never wanted to abandon the pure joy of it. Running will always be a part of my life until I physically can't do it any longer.

One of the reasons why I love it so much now is that for many years, despite showing early promise, I struggled to put any consistent training together. In 1990 I followed up my 1988 junior (Under-15) double at the AAAs by winning the intermediate (Under-17) 800m and 1,500m titles. But at the end of the track season I had severe pain in my feet and my Achilles, and calf problems too. First I was reduced to hobbling, then I had to stop altogether. I was diagnosed with hallux rigidus, more commonly known as arthritis of the main joint of the big toe in the ball of the foot, caused by a wearing out of the joint surfaces. It meant that I had a massively reduced range in my big toes, especially on the right. In order to run freely and mechanically correctly you need a good range in your big toe to achieve 'toe off' – the phrase used to describe the movement through which your foot leaves the ground via the ball of the foot. Owing to the hallux rigidus, I could only get the range I needed to toe off by coming off the ground with my foot in a position of excessive pronation. (In layman's terms, excessive pronation is when your foot rolls in too much after landing.) This had the knock-on effect of causing injuries in my lower legs and affecting how efficiently I can run, too.

It became clear that in order ever to run again, I had to work hard to get movement in both big toes to a functional range. Because I'd had some pleasing performances as a junior, I was referred to the Olympic Medical Centre at Northwick Park Hospital, and they recommended orthopaedic surgery in Exeter. I had an operation on my right foot to improve the range, but it was an extremely painful recovery. I was on crutches for a while and it took a long time to settle down. Little things would cause massive setbacks. During these years I saw many podiatrists, some very good ones who were helpful at that particular point in my career. However, I became a bit troubled by the huge differences in the various orthotic inserts I would receive to put in my shoes. I accumulated piles of them, and was left confused about which ones I should be putting in my running shoes for the best results.

Gav and I had not long been going out when I developed this string of injuries. Over the next few years, it was one step (or limp) forward, two steps back, over and over again. If someone had told me it would be seven years before I was back in competition again, I'm not sure I would have believed them. Throughout my career I've often heard the phrase 'you'll never run competitively again' – and it has always gone over the top of my head. I was blinkered in my focus on overcoming each setback as it arose. I can't believe I lost the entire seasons of 1991 to 1996 inclusive to a catalogue of injuries. When I was sidelined, I went along to the club because Gav remained in training and was full-on with his running up to 1994. It was important to feel involved in the club, and I loved being there to support him.

On the telly, I saw the runners who inspired me achieve their dreams. I watched Sonia O'Sullivan's incredible medal haul: silver in the 1993 World Championships in Stuttgart, followed by golds in the 1994 Euros and the 1995 Worlds in Gothenburg, where Kelly Holmes won the silver. Where was I? Working hard to battle against injury setbacks and undoubtedly busy with other things in life. I never gave up on the dream of seeing what I could achieve if I could train consistently. It was always in my mind. I would run for a few weeks or months then the problems would recur. I'd be forced to stop again. After the pain subsided, I'd start running again and then the injuries would return. Again and again. I felt trapped in the cycle, but I refused to let go of my passion for running.

Gav couldn't believe what I was putting myself through. 'You could be doing yourself long-term damage,' he'd say. I was having none of that and wouldn't even discuss it. I had only one agenda – and that was to run. I just wanted to regain that incredible sensation of running freely at speed. It was all about not letting go of that precious discovery I had made as a young schoolgirl. In that intense period from 1988 to 1990, running had come to be such a big part of who I was. I was determined never to lose the ability to run, to experience the exhilaration of racing and all the other positive things that running brought to my life. Gav saw that I was committed to regaining full fitness. 'Stubbornly' committed, he'd probably say – and he was 100 per cent supportive in helping me. I never thought that it wasn't meant to be. I always thought if I worked hard enough, I could get it back. I was so passionate about wanting to run and finding out what I could do that I didn't consider doing anything other than trying to get back. I never made a conscious plan or gave myself ultimatums, I just kept at it.

To an extent, injuries are part of sport but training young athletes is often a delicate matter. Determined youngsters are going to have that inner drive to want to do well. Allowing them to achieve some of their goals in a safe, sensible way will help keep them interested in the sport. However, you have to know when to back off, and monitor their training carefully to ensure it is age-appropriate and suitable for their stage of growth and development. It is also important to know when to tell them to stop overdoing things. As a teenager I trained hard. I put a lot of pressure on myself. As I could see my times getting better and better, I worked harder and harder to continue the trend of personal bests. It's part of my character to want evidence of improvement as a result of work I've put into something.

I enjoy working towards a goal. In my training, in my racing – and in my period later as a physiotherapist – I love the reward of an improved measurable outcome. In those sessions, running with the men in the club, I pushed probably more than I should have done. When I was set a task in training I always wanted to do it to the best of my ability. In a way, that pushing, that finding out what I had in me, nurtured my love of the sport.

While I was resigned to the struggle to recover from my foot injury, I gained a place to study Maths at Birmingham University following my A levels. I loved maths and science at school – subjects with measurable outcomes, I guess. I was in the car with Mike Down, who was Gav's coach – and later became mine – coming back from a race in Stratford that Gav had competed in when the conversation turned to university. I said I wasn't sure about choosing maths. I wanted a career I felt passionate about; I wanted to help people. I said I wished I'd applied to do physiotherapy – I'd seen so many by then I could see it was rewarding work and, through my own injuries, I'd become interested in the way the human body works. It was officially too late to change, but Mike said, 'No, no, you must just write lots of letters.' Inspired by his words, I did just that and was invited for an interview at the Avon and Gloucestershire College of Health in Bristol. They had two places left, which four of us interviewed for. The interview was quite scary. I had accepted the idea of taking a year off in order to swap courses – and couldn't believe it when they told me then and there that I'd got a place to study for a physiotherapy degree that term. Dad took me for a meal in the Harvester pub to celebrate, and in September 1992 I started the three-year course.

*

Despite the thwarted attempts to get back into competitive running, my university years were very happy and busy. On my course I had a good friend, Julia, who later became my bridesmaid. The course inevitably had some practical elements to it. On our first day, they threw us in at the deep end to get the embarrassment over and done with, asking us to take off our clothes down to our underwear to identify certain points on the body! The nature of my degree course meant I was on work placements all over the west of England, particularly down in Cornwall, it seemed. Because I was from the south-west, I was given all the jobs in that area – Truro and then up north as far as Hereford as well – so it wasn't easy to keep doing the rehabilitation work needed to get over the latest setback, but I was definitely not one to wallow in the frustration of my running injuries. A physio degree didn't always allow for a typical student lifestyle. With the placements, I was essentially doing a full-time job while also trying to do my reading, my dissertation and other projects. I sometimes looked with envy at friends who had a few lectures a week and then just had to write essays in their own time. Typed essays and paperwork were a requirement of my course, but this was before anyone had their own laptops or tablets. I'd have to travel daily to my placement, get back to university, spend all night in the computer room bashing away at a keyboard, grab a bit of sleep, then hop straight on a train again the next morning. It entailed lots of classic all-nighters, with a nine-to-five job thrown in for good measure. However, we made sure we fitted in the hugely important crazy student nights out in Bristol during the times when we were all back from our placements. We certainly knew how to work hard and play hard!

My student life was as far as you can imagine from that of a professional athlete. At the end of my first year at college, Gav and I spent the summer driving around France in our old red Ford Fiesta. We didn't have credit or debit cards. We just took a wodge of cash to get us around our planned route on a tight fuel budget. We pledged not to buy food, or eat out, so we crammed the car boot with tins of baked beans, tuna and spaghetti hoops, alongside a camping stove and a two-man tent. Our planned route would take us through Brittany and on to the Loire Valley, turning south-west towards Geneva and then back via north-west Italy and the South of France to Perpignan, and finally looping back to Brittany via Toulouse. We hadn't budgeted for campsites either so we also took plenty of bin liners and tape to cover the windows when we pulled over somewhere and slept in the car. It became apparent the old Fiesta was not as fuel-efficient as we'd calculated, which messed up our careful currency plans. These were the days before the Euro or twenty-four-hour service stations, and we only had a certain amount of francs and lira. There were several nightmare moments when we were about to run out of fuel and the road in the Maritime Alps forced us back into Italy with no lira. It was crazy.

Our pace was slower than we'd plotted too, because we couldn't afford toll roads. We'd drive at night or early in the morning to make up time, then get very tired. Once, when we'd woken at 5 a.m. to hit the roads before rush hour, Gav instinctively went out on the British and wrong side of the road. Neither of us noticed until a car came in the other direction, honking and flashing its lights, and we swerved and mounted the kerb to escape an impact. The car kept breaking down too, always in an awkward situation. We were in a long queue of traffic on a narrow road going up a steep gradient towards the Matterhorn when it overheated and abruptly stopped. To the amusement of the line of drivers behind us, we somehow manoeuvred it 180 degrees and then free-wheeled down the entire winding mountain road.

As Gav drove, I was continually re-calculating our expected costs against a dwindling budget. It was very stressful at times, but a true adventure. Would we have enough to get home? In the end we bailed out early in the Pyrenees, and bypassed the Bay of Biscay coastline, to ensure we'd get back to the UK. It was all good fun – and I'm so grateful I had those authentic student experiences while I was too injured to pursue my running – although one incident was far more sinister. We'd pulled into a garage to fill up the car and Gav went in to pay. He whipped out his wallet, which at that stage was still bulging with cash, and when he asked the garage attendant for directions to our next destination, the guy behind him in the queue said he and his mates were going that way so we could follow them. It was dark. We didn't suspect a thing. We kept driving on their tail and followed them down a turning, which led into a deserted industrial area. They stopped and all got out of their car, approaching us with menace. It suddenly became clear they intended to rob us. I don't know how Gav stayed so calm as he quickly did a three-point turn and we raced away.

When I felt frustrated about my injury woes, I'd always get support from Gav and I kept in touch with Tony, who'd also keep me chipper. He wanted me to know he was always on the end of the phone. His calm words of encouragement were always reassuring to hear. For as long as I'd known him, Tony had always worn thick pebble glasses. I knew that his sight had been getting poorer over the years, but during one of our phone calls he confessed he'd been told he would soon be blind and that he worried that he might never see me race again. That was heartbreaking for me to hear him say. I discussed it with Gav and we came up with a plan for me to run a 3k in the Women's Southern League in Exeter so that Tony could see me run one last time. I was determined to stay fit enough to see this through. By now, his vision had deteriorated to the extent that he could just about see me when I ran past him, but he couldn't register the rest of the action around a lap.

We all went to the meet together and I felt so emotional running past him, I really went for it, going off far too fast for my level of fitness. I was blowing up big time by the end, but I won and came across to ask if he'd seen me. 'Yes,' he nodded. 'I knew you'd be in the front.' Then we both broke down and cried.

Ever my motivator, Tony quietly remarked that he would still be able to see me on a large-screen TV.

'Right,' I joked. 'I better get selected for the GB team again!'

I said it in jest, but it was a goal that stayed at the back of my mind while I continued enjoying a normal student life, burning the candle at both ends. If I had been somewhere that had a serious athletics set-up, I might not have had so much 'student' fun. I loved the challenge of trying to fit in my early run while travelling to placements and doing all-nighter essays. I recall running early then walking an hour to my placement at a hospital in Taunton, my wet hair frozen; or arriving somewhere early and finding a local park to do a quick run before I started work. I tried to do my running in any spare time I could find because I loved it.

I was busy studying for my degree, away a lot on placements, and it was very important for me to see Gav. Injuries permitting,

I ran with him in Mike Down's group when I was back from placements. Mike was our coach during our time in Bristol and I still raced now and again while at university. He was a great support and arranged for me to do hours of 'aqua jogging' at the Bristol University pool. My Aquabelt – the buoyancy device, which suspends you at shoulder level in water so you can transfer a land-based programme to a non-impact session in the pool – became one of most trusted pieces of kit.

I didn't have enough understanding of my injury problems to deal with them effectively at this stage, but I remained determined. I craved getting in a solid block of training to see if I could reach a good level. I never considered giving up. With physio placements all over the place and continual niggles, I struggled to put together a logical training programme. But I have so many good memories of running when I could and the inner drive to keep going for it was always there.

CHAPTER 6
Engaged and Married

On 21 December 1992, when I was nineteen and Gav was twenty-one, we became engaged. Unbeknownst to me, Gav had bought a ring and carried it around with him for about a month. He wanted somewhere special for the proposal and then remembered this romantic spot on Dartmoor called Dr Blackall's Drive. In the 1880s, the doctor from Exeter who owned nearby Spitchwick Manor cleared a drive above the beautiful Dart Valley to make it possible to enjoy the remarkable views. So Gav and I hiked along this two-mile stretch of stony pathway on the moors and sat on a rocky outcrop overlooking the deep, forested, V-shaped valley with the river sparkling in the sun at the bottom. Gav pulled out a ring from amongst the sandwiches and flask he'd packed, and went down on one knee. He popped the question. It was a lovely, romantic moment and I said yes immediately.

Not all Gav's romantic gestures had such perfect endings. One time, he was taking me to Ilsington on Dartmoor, to see the Old School House where he and his brother Alex were born. He borrowed his parents' brand-new blue Ford Fiesta – the only new car they have ever bought – and we arrived in the picturesque village, with its narrow lanes and rugged free-stone walls. In his enthusiasm to point out the window of the room where he and his brother were born, Gav drove too close to the garden wall and we heard the unmistakable sound of metal on rock as the entire left side of the car scraped along the granite wall. He couldn't believe it. After manoeuvring it away from the wall, he got out and ran his hands down the paintwork to inspect the damage. I knew it was bad when he buried his face in his hands with horror. When we got back to his parents' house, Gav's mum said she guessed as soon as she saw him that he'd done something to the car because his face was still smeared with blue paint!

We started arranging things for our big day while we were still at university. There we were, still studying, cramming for our final exams; arranging weddings was hardly top of most people's priority lists at that stage in life. And we were incredibly fortunate because our parents helped out too. In the lead up, Gav and I were both busy with summer jobs. In fact, we always had summer jobs and evening jobs. At one point we both worked at Burger King in Exeter. Strangely enough, I did enjoy the challenge of making burgers as fast as I could. Gav often did labouring work, too, and I worked at a neural rehabilitation centre.

We got married the summer after I finished at university, in 1995, when I was twenty-one and Gav was twenty-three. It seems a frighteningly long time ago now, as we celebrated our twentieth anniversary in 2015. As we were both from Devon, and we both still felt very much that it was home, we planned a traditional white wedding in my local village church in Feniton. I was so happy to be marrying the man with whom I had fallen in love at a young age. The service was followed by a reception in Escot House, a private Grade II listed nineteenth-century house with surrounding parkland designed by Capability Brown. It is now a tourist attraction, open to the public – and our daughter Emily loves visiting the red squirrel reserve – but in 1995 it was the closest wedding venue to Feniton and somewhere I'd often run past. The setting was indisputably grand – and we had a vintage car to match – but we made it a fun wedding with all our friends from university as well as friends from home and our families. Our bridesmaids were my childhood friend Becca (just three weeks after being hers) and my college friend Julia, and our brothers did a brilliant job as ushers. Everyone enjoyed the speeches – my dad reminiscing over my early years and Gav having everyone in fits of laughter as he scrolled through his notes saying, 'No, I can't say that,' as he lost his nerve to tell his pre-planned jokes. Our best man was Chi Man Woo, our great friend from Hong Kong. He was Gav's university friend and arrived speaking only a few words of English but went on achieve a first-class degree. His speech was hilarious thanks to his foreign sense of humour. We all danced until the early hours of the morning; our guests probably thought we were never going to leave. We had a fantastic send-off and set off on honeymoon, but then had to get the driver to return a few minutes later as we had forgotten our hotel key. Just a bit embarrassing . . .

We went on honeymoon to the beautiful village and resort of Ölüdeniz on the Turquoise Coast of south-west Turkey. With a lovely sandy beach next to a lagoon perfect for swimming, it was quiet and beautiful. The area has since become much more developed, but there was only one hotel to stay in when we were there. We had fun exploring and driving miles and miles up into the mountains on a rickety old truck to go paragliding. In tandem with an instructor, we had to pretty much run off the cliff and sail down above incredible landscape only to land a short while later practically outside our hotel room.

That September I started a job as a newly qualified physiotherapist at the Royal United Hospital in Bath. They were fun times. I loved the camaraderie of the physio department, the laughter in the staff room during breaks. Gav, meanwhile, had secured a job as a quantity surveyor, and together we rented a flat. It seemed like this was it: jobs, rent, a grown-up life. Running properly seemed like a distant dream. But during those lost years, memories of winning the English Schools and Amateur Athletic Association titles as a teenager kept that flame burning in the back of my mind. It never went away; it was always there. If I could win those titles, setting new records, maybe I had the innate talent to make it as senior athlete? If I had that potential, if I had that ability, I could find it again, couldn't I? I could push harder, go faster, be stronger. That little voice, that intrigue in the back of my mind, counted for a lot. It made me curious. What if I try again? What if I get through these injuries and put a good season's training together? Maybe I could make it. Maybe not. But would I ever want to look back and think I didn't try? Who wants to look back at their life and see a big, gaping missed opportunity? I desperately wanted to know. Could I make it as an athlete? Could I represent my country as a senior athlete?

When I started studying for my degree, my running 'career' – if you can call my schoolgirl exploits that – was over before it had fully launched. So when I started out as a physio at the Royal United Hospital in Bath I thought that would most likely occupy the rest of my working life. I had lovely colleagues who soon became good friends. On Friday evenings we'd all go to the Old Crown pub and have the same meal every week, cod and chips, or 'whale and chips' as we referred to it because of the generous portions. Then we'd head out to a club afterwards. It was a Friday-night ritual and a lovely team environment with Ross and Dana, Kol and Mel, Dave, Sally, Celia . . . I found the physio work rewarding. As with my running, and my own bid to regain fitness, I loved seeing physical improvement in my patients, who weren't all seeing me for sports physio treatments. If I'd continued and was working as a physio now, I'd have liked to specialise in rehabilitation, treating patients who had had a stroke or a head injury. In that role, you have the chance to truly make a difference to people's lives. You might be able to help them stand or walk again, or relieve their pain and frustration. Watching people start to regain function is very rewarding and you can see the improvement as you work.

So there we were, Gav and I, in our twenties. We had our degrees, we had career paths, we were married, we rented a tiny flat right off the Royal Crescent in Bath, we'd saved our money. The natural next step was to buy a house, to fill one day with kids. When I'd been working as a physio for eighteen months, we thought we ought to get on the property ladder. So we embarked on a house-hunting mission and found a lovely place near Bath, in Midsomer Norton. It all happened so fast. We put in an offer, which the owner accepted. And then something made us think twice.

Earlier that year, I'd managed to put together a few weeks of training, and raced the 1,500m at the National Championships. I wasn't fully fit. I was still in the midst of those long and frustrating stop/start years of injury, but I finished in a time of 4:21. It was not a notable time compared to elite runners, but it was an eye-opener. Gav reckoned that, with proper consistent training, I'd run at least 10 to 15 seconds quicker, and that could earn me qualification at elite level. He thought I had the talent to improve and make it as a professional. One morning we looked at each other over the mortgage offers and surveys and letters from estate agents piling up on the kitchen table and said, 'What are we doing? We're still so young! Is this it?' Buying a house and getting tied into a mortgage might be the natural next step, but we didn't have to do it just yet, did we? Shouldn't we go and live a little? Explore all life's possibilities? Before we knew it, we'd quit our jobs, booked round-the-world flights and packed a couple of rucksacks.

I was twenty-three, relatively injury-free and managing to run more consistently than in previous months. I relished every stride. I would go out with Gav, rekindling that love of running now that every trip out in my trainers wasn't accompanied by nerves about how much it would hurt, or whether I'd have to limp back, defeated once more. After all the years I'd been out of the sport, I had been embarrassed to tell my physiotherapy colleagues and Bristol friends that my secret ambition was to be a professional athlete. After so long out, and only my schoolgirl exploits to refer to, I felt a bit of a fraud. The 4:21 was the catalyst that drove us to go travelling, not just for the adventure, but also to work hard together to see how much I could improve. We'd be giving it a go under the radar, behind the pretence of a once-in-a-lifetime travel adventure, and we would come back knowing which way our life would go. By setting off on a round-the-world trip, we were embarking on our own weird version of a warm-weather training camp, without fully admitting to ourselves that that's what we were doing. It was a win-win situation. If it didn't work out, and the training came to nothing – we'd have had an amazing trip, spent some wonderful time together, and return home with memories and photos to bore people with for the rest of our lives. Secretly, though, we had an inner belief that we could make it happen.

CHAPTER 7

Round the World

Our round-the-world ticket took us to Hong Kong, Bali, Australia, New Zealand, Fiji and Hawaii. We deliberately chose places we knew we could train – we weren't about to pilot as a duo up the Amazon or climb the Himalayas – but the travel meant any training we did had to be very spontaneous. We moved on almost every day, never lingering in one place for more than a night or two. There was so much of the world to see. We blew all our savings on that trip, and yet we didn't feel pain in spending it. Every day we were training in stunning landscapes and it was truly inspiring. We'd wake up and run a new route into the unknown, wondering what was around the corner. I'd grown up running through tiny, winding Devon lanes with high hedgerows, past fields with sheep and cattle. On our travels, we saw so much more by running than we would have on the tourist trail. Walking and talking you're sounding out an alarm, but running silently and light on our feet, we could explore in stealth. We startled kangaroos in a clearing near Byron Bay in Australia, passed a wombat at the same spot each time we did a lap on Wilsons Promontary peninsula and came across a clumsy echidna (a tiny spiky anteater) near Melbourne.

Was it a professional way to give athletics a good shot? Of course not. In Bali, we went to the Sacred Monkey Forest Sanctuary in Ubud where Gav bought some bananas – classic athlete's fuel – which we lost when a huge monkey swung from a tree, knocked Gav to the ground and made off with the bananas. On Fraser Island, off the coast of Queensland, a dingo stole our food supplies and we had nothing to eat for a few days. But we weren't bothered; we just fell into the relaxed vibe of the backpacking lifestyle. We didn't always know where we would be, whether we could train there, what the terrain would be like. There was no set schedule of a track session here, a long run there, a recovery run in the middle . . . We'd travel, and when we saw a good spot we'd put down our bags and run. We had running shoes, what else did we need? We ran in all sorts of conditions: high humidity in Indonesia and Fiji, stifling dry heat in the Australian Outback, cool southern alpine air in New Zealand. In Australia we ran in the arid red-soil terrain of the centre, in the tropical north-eastern landscape around Cairns, along beaches on the Gold Coast, through the rolling green landscapes of Victoria. In remote spots, we'd laugh about the amount of teeming wildlife apparently waiting to kill us – from box jellyfish to salt-water crocodiles, funnel-web spiders to all sorts of venomous snakes.

For most of the time we were away we were lugging our big rucksacks around on buses or trains, which must have constituted some strength training. In New Zealand we hired a car for a month to get around and immerse ourselves in an authentic experience of the wilderness. If we saw a sports field, we'd stop the car and dash out to do a session. New Zealand was particularly wonderful, not just for its stunning natural beauty, but because the huge national parks were criss-crossed with well-mapped and -signposted hiking routes so we could easily assess our mileage. We would pick a walking trail, run it, then jump back in the car, find a campsite, put up the tent and cook a meal to eat under the stars. In the morning, we might crawl out of our tiny tent, have a sip of water and then set off again for another run. For me, that was the hardest bit – I need a cup of coffee at the very least before I run!

Sometimes our routes were urban. One day in Sydney, we'd had a busy day sightseeing, undertaking the kind of slow plod from sight to sight that you do around cities that leaves you more knackered than running miles. We were trudging on weary feet back to our hostel when we saw a lovely hilly park, beautifully lit up by the street lighting. We couldn't resist that kind of opportunity so down went our bags, and we did a hill session there and then even though it was ten o'clock at night. God knows what passers-by must have thought when they saw these two mad people sprinting up and down a hill with rucksacks as markers when most people were turning into bed. Another memorable hill session was in Indonesia – largely because it wasn't a hill but a volcano. An inactive one, I hasten to add, though we did joke that if it had been likely to erupt, that might have made us pick up our pace.

Sometimes on that trip it was tough to run owing to perilously steep or tricky surfaces, or it was just ridiculously hot – but we took the view that anything harder would toughen us up. When we visited Ayers Rock – Uluru – we couldn't resist breaking into a run there too at 4.30 a.m. in the morning. The other people in our group thought we were completely nuts.

None of those sessions had anything to do with paces or measuring distances; there were no GPS watches back then. We were simply working away on fitness and getting miles in our legs. Every interval session we did was based on 'perceived effort' – working as hard as we could for a set period, but not bothering to work out what our actual pace was. That would be meaningless anyway when the terrain or gradient or surface was different from one day to the next. Over the last couple of years Gav had moved away from running seriously himself to focusing on helping me with my training.

Our running was interrupted by trips – a few amazing days learning how to sail on an America's Cup yacht – and plenty of hangovers, but our travels didn't all go entirely smoothly. We were staying on an island off Fiji when a cyclone hit and we had to hole up in our little beach hut. The setting – just metres from the azure sea – was beautiful, even if the accommodation was definitely backpackers' budget style. The cyclone, funnily enough, was called Cyclone Gavin. Before the storm hit, the locals were laughing about this chap called Gavin who was bringing in his own cyclone, but the experience was terrifying, and heartbreaking ultimately for many of the islanders who lost property or their livelihoods. Sadly there was also loss of life. The sound of a cyclone is intensely physical. We were huddled under a bed, pushed up against a wall, while wind-bowled coconuts battered the roof of our tiny beach hut. The force of the winds whipped the walls so loudly you had to yell in each other's ears to be heard. I was terrified we might die, and we were moved to scribble notes to our families in case we didn't survive. Once the cyclone passed, the morning broke with a near-supernatural calmness, and we emerged to find utter destruction on our paradise island. The jetty had disappeared and the beach was gone, the sand sucked away by the wind. We were pained to see many of the islanders' fishing boats minced, floating like thousands of pieces of driftwood. We were stranded on the island for two or three days as there was no boat to get back, with only cyclone-harvested coconuts to eat, though our travails were nothing compared to the islanders who lost everything.

We also got lost once or twice on our runs. How could we not, when we were running new, unfamiliar routes every single day? But we felt young and free. We had each other and no dependents, so if we became lost for several hours – as we did in the rugged Blue Mountains, west of Sydney – we shrugged as we sought to find a way out. There are worse places to get lost than in a stunning landscape of steep cliffs, eucalyptus forests and waterfalls. The worst case of disorientation came on Mount Batur, an active volcano in Indonesia notable for rock formations made of solidified lava flows from previous eruptions. We chose not to have a guide in order to save money. How hard could it be, we thought, to walk to the top and back? Running up was fine; we found a nice stretch ideal for hill reps so did a session. Coming back down was something else. The lava flows resembled natural paths so we followed one down the side of the mountain only to discover a sheer drop where the flow ended. So up we went again, back to the top, and down again on another stretch of rocky trail that looked more likely. Same thing: another precipitous drop at the bottom. Up and down we went until it started getting dark and we began to fear we'd be spending the night on that volcano, though at least it was warm, and we had water. Eventually we found a way to descend to the treeline, picking our way through the deep forest in pitch dark to find our hired jeep.

One of the things that made the trip so special was the feeling of being cut off from our conventional everyday lives and learning to become more self-reliant – though sometimes that was a bit hairy. North of Cairns, for example, we had an incident that still makes me shiver to recall. Strolling from our campsite we happened upon a beautiful deserted beach. Fringed by palm trees straight out of an exotic holiday brochure, it was idyllic. We set up camp for the day, laying down towels and sarongs to read and relax and doze in the sun. It was a wonderful lazy day, lying there half asleep. When the campsite owner asked us where we'd been that day, and we told him, he went crazy: 'You bloody idiots! The beach is off-limits. Didn't you see my signs? A f***ing saltie has been prowling up and down it all week.'

We were more than merely physically remote. There were no mobile phones then. We sometimes bought phone cards, so we could try to find a phone box to occasionally call home and let our parents know we were having a great time. We spent our first Christmas away from our families – in sunscreen, swimming costumes, shorts and flip-flops in Australia. We had Christmas dinner on the beach, eating our packed Christmas lunch off the back of a surfboard, and spent the afternoon kayaking and paddling out to a sandbar covered in pelicans. That was such a novelty. We saw in the New Year – 1997 – at Surfers Paradise, having a great time listening to tribute bands of Nirvana and Pearl Jam as we were sprayed with foam from a giant foam machine. Little did I know that three years later, I would be back on the very same beach, for an Olympic holding camp.

In Sydney we made a point of seeking out the area in the suburb of Homebush where construction was under way on the Olympic Stadium for the Sydney Games in 2000. Some facilities had already been built, such as the warm-up track and the Olympic pool, but the main stadium was still a building site. We walked up to the outer fence of the construction site to have a good look at the excavations, and try to work out what was going where. We weren't drawn there purely out of curiosity. I was looking through the wiring wondering if there was any chance, any possibility, that I might be able to make it to Sydney in a GB vest. Gav and I discussed it, but, standing there with a backpack, it seemed so unlikely. And yet I had been running all over the world so far without a hitch; I seemed to be injury-free at last. I peered through the fence, taking my time to visualise competing there, soaking up the 'work in progress' as motivation. As an athlete, I was a work in progress too, hoping to be ready in time.

I was outside that fence looking in, but with such a positive frame of mind. I knew I was getting fitter and stronger, even though I had no way of measuring how much fitness I had attained out on the road, up hills and mountains and volcanoes. We rarely found any measurable distance we could time a run over consistently. Our intent was to factor in running every day, but our plans had been interrupted by trips at sea, storms, long flights and great nights out. I wasn't living the clean life of a professional athlete. I didn't let up on late nights and having fun. I had been held back for a day here, or a few days there. This, in itself, was good as it allowed my body time to condition and adapt before pushing on again. A relaxed, gradual fitness programme over six months was exactly what an over-enthusiastic runner like me needed.

We arrived back home in the spring, cunningly missing the worst of the winter weather. Nevertheless, Britain looked dismal and grey when we left the airport terminal. Anyone who has been away for a long stretch of time will know that slightly disorientating feeling. You're glad to be home, to see all the people you missed, hug your family, get back into the normal routines, but part of you pines for golden sunlight and warmth and a landscape that changes every day from one glorious view to the next. On our first night home we knocked back the Fiji Rum – 58 per cent proof – pleased to see our family again, saying how great it was to be back. Waking up with a pounding head and looking out at the rain could not have been more of a contrast from the sun and surf of our last stop, Hawaii. What felt like an eternity when I was away suddenly felt like a few weeks. Instead of golden beaches and crystal-clear waters and lush forests, we had England in April: rain, more rain, and just for a change, plenty of drizzle.

To add to that feeling of dislocation, I didn't have a 'normal routine' to slot back into. Gav and I had made the decision that I would keep training full time when we returned – something he supported 100 per cent. The secret underlying motive of our trip had been to see if I could keep pushing my fitness, and that had gone well, but was it realistic to transfer that on to the track? Gav wrote hundreds of letters and found a job pretty much straightaway, working as a quantity surveyor, so I had to get down to work, too, and hit the track. I had made myself a window of opportunity and wanted to give myself the best chance of making it. If I went through the stress of applying for jobs, and if I then got a new job and gave it my all, I may have wasted that opportunity. It was an awkward time. People would ask if I'd found work yet, and I found it difficult to answer. I didn't feel comfortable sharing my dream.

Our backpacking trip was the catalyst I needed to reboot my running career, but it seems crazy to me to think that six months after setting off full of tentative hope about my fitness, I came back in athlete mode. What next? I was well aware that I would need to get a qualifying time in order to have a shot at the

1997 World Championships in Athens in the summer. If it was a huge jump in mindset, it would also require a parallel jump in my personal best: the qualifying time was 11 seconds quicker than I'd ever run. Was Gav right in thinking I could whittle down that pre-travelling milestone time of 4:21 to the required 4:10? When I was a junior, I used to think the times run by the senior athletes were superhuman. So while Gav and I talked about having a shot at it, I didn't feel over-confident. I was optimistic but equally wondering whether it was a realistic possibility. And then I'd summon up the memory of looking through that fence in Sydney, daring to dream . . .

CHAPTER 8

An Elite Athlete

I hadn't so much as seen a track in months, let alone run on one. However fit I'd become, however many miles I'd clocked up and however many hill repeats up volcanoes or in parks and in woods I could count, I was not going to be sharp enough to run a good 1,500m on a track without more focused, specialist speed training. Fitness is one thing; race fitness is something else altogether. Knowing I needed to concentrate on that, I rejoined Mike Down's training group with the specific mission of gaining a place and a qualifying time for the 1997 World Championships. From the outside, my form didn't look too bad because I was in pretty good shape but I desperately needed to make a massive mental adjustment from backpacker to bona-fide athlete. I worked hard in the sessions that Mike set me. He has since said complimentary things about how quickly I seemed to progress from what must have seemed like an enthusiastic amateur to a pro in a few months. But it didn't feel that way. I felt a bit strange training like a full-time athlete when I was so far from recognised as one, but I remained focused. Gav jollied me through this period of self-doubt. 'Oh come on,' he'd say, 'let's just give it two or three months to see what happens.'

Of course he was right and I am so grateful to him. He always believed in me. I sharpened up that track fitness with endless reps and training sessions. To improve as a distance runner, you need to build shorter, faster intervals of running into your schedule as well as doing the long runs to get miles under your belt. You also need to do strength and conditioning work, and core work. It felt like an eternity but my work began to translate into decent times. I put my fitness to the test at a couple of races in the UK, and then one low-key track meeting in Germany where I was pleased to run a personal best. My times came down: 4:18, 4:15, 4:15, 4:11 . . . My target was 4:10. I did my first two races back in British Milers Club meetings. The BMC, founded by the legendary Frank Horwill in 1963, is an institution in British distance running. They hold fantastic meetings with a system of graded races. In this way, many athletes get a chance to run personal bests and qualifying times, and perhaps achieve a time that gets them accepted into an international meeting for the first time. Their races were to prove helpful at many points during my career. I was feeling my way back into high-level competition and the really big test and opportunity would be a meeting at the Don Valley Stadium in Sheffield on 29 June.

That 1,500m was a fascinating race to be part of. Unlike my teenage self, who always wanted to get to the front and push and push myself to cross the line first, I was aware I had come with a job to do: to chase a qualifying time for the World Championships. And now, as a senior, I was sure to be shocked by the standard of competition. No matter what went on around me, I was running my own race, strictly keeping to my lap times. Kelly Holmes was there, having won bronze and silver in the 800m and 1,500m respectively at the previous World

Championships in Gothenburg. She was the golden girl of middle-distance running and when the gun went, lots of the field went off with her. The race was tough. It was my first ever grand prix; the standard was high. I had to dig deep. On the home straight I felt like I was swimming, pushing so hard my legs were blowing up with lactic acid build-up. The girls who had gone off with Kelly folded and I came from way back to clinch third in a time of 4:07.28 – a time that transformed me from 'young girl with promise blighted by injuries' to an elite runner with a qualifying time for the World Championships. I could scarcely believe it!

There was a real buzz surrounding the race result because Kelly set a new British record, but that was a perfect backdrop for my own jubilant celebration. I was exhilarated, exhausted, ecstatic – and completely under the radar. I wasn't mentioned by the commentators because of the excitement of Kelly breaking the record, which is always a cause for universal celebration, so it was a double celebration for me. I had qualified for my first senior championships at the age of twenty-four! After six long years of battling, of refusing to let go of my passion for running, that last all-out effort felt just awesome. Rejoicing afterwards with Gav and Mike, I felt I had rediscovered the real me again: enduring pain, absorbing exhaustion, gasping for air, and loving every second of it. I came from God knows how many metres back to cross the line in third place, but I had come from so much further back psychologically to even run that race in Sheffield. This is what I wanted so much. This is why I had refused to stop.

June 29: I will always remember that date. It was so significant. That was the day I showed myself that a career in athletics was possible. I was no longer a junior who had shown talent or a club runner with secret aspirations. I could run at the standard required to be an international athlete. I spent the following week floating on cloud nine. I'd do something ordinary, like drive to the shops, and be overcome with a surreal realisation of what I had achieved. I still hadn't been selected but I had put in a performance of the standard required, and Kelly and I were the only runners to have run that time that year. A couple of weeks later I won my first ever national championship and I was in the team.

And so, eight years after the one and only time I had worn a GB vest, as a fifteen-year-old selected for the U20 team in 1989, I would coincidentally head back to the same city – Athens – to make my senior GB debut. Apart from that one race at a very young age, I had missed the entire U20 scene. I had missed being on a steady trajectory, gradually watching my PBs come down from the 4:27 I ran to break the GB U15 record. For me there had been no incremental yearly progression. But somehow I had achieved something I feared for a long time might be a crazy pipe dream. My first senior GB selection was actually as reserve for the European Cup in Munich in June. The squad included a reserve for the 1,500m, 3,000m and 5,000m and that was my role: I would warm up on track for every event in case any GB athlete had the misfortune to tear a muscle and pull up in pain during their warm up. It would be a dry run for the World Championships, a valuable familiarising process as I didn't know the ropes at all; I couldn't have planned it better.

Getting on the plane, for once travelling on my own, I looked around and saw people I recognised, the faces of my athletics heroes – Sally Gunnell, Colin Jackson, Roger Black. While I recognised virtually everyone, I didn't actually know a soul so it was really daunting. I was aware that my life had been very different from these professionals who knew each other well. It was terrifying, especially when I was told I'd been allocated to share a room with Kelly Holmes. I'd watched her on the TV, run behind her as she broke the British record in Sheffield, but I'd never actually met her properly. It was quite a daunting prospect to be rooming with her. She was on a later flight out to Munich, and I sat on my hotel bed, fidgeting, twiddling my thumbs nervously, not knowing what to do. I was almost hiding in my room because I had no one to hang around with. Every time I walked out of the room I'd see famous athletes chatting to each other. Everyone was friendly but I was self-conscious, feeling a bit of a fraud again, a little voice in my head saying, 'What are *you* doing here?'

After what seemed like hours, I heard the key in the door. My heart was pounding. There was Kelly! And of course, I'd had no reason to be nervous. She was lovely, incredibly friendly and supportive from the very second she walked in – and indeed always has been. Kelly had a reputation for being a great team player. Even when she was out winning races and setting amazing times, she'd think of her teammates with nice gestures like putting good-luck messages under their doors. She went out of her way to make sure I was okay on that trip and that I felt welcome. Seven years later when she had won the first of her two gold medals at the 2004 Olympics, we would celebrate together with a mug of cocoa. (The champagne had to wait until after her second.) The competition went well and the men's team won the cup, partly thanks to the heroic effort of my friend Rob Hough, who was the surprise winner of the steeplechase.

Later that summer, I could hardly absorb the fact I was a member of the GB team going to the World Championships. My family flew to Athens to support me. I was incredibly nervous, and it was a great comfort to see them watch me go through my strides and running drills through the wire fence that surrounded the warm-up area, though I was so overwhelmed by the enormity of the occasion that I could hardly function on a social level and actually talk to them. As I was led out for my heat, I saw the awful sight of Kelly pull up – clearly in pain – with an injury. She was running in the heat before mine, and it was a devastating scene. It was such a big deal for her and for the team because she was favourite to win. I was shocked but had no time to absorb the drama because I was lining up for the next heat. And it was tough. I did get through to the semi-final, but I remember having to be more tactically savvy than ever before. I was trying to get it right, to bravely put in a drive with 800m to go in order to cope with the fast finishers. I'd never raced in such a crowded field. I was boxed in. There seemed to be so many girls around me. Everything unfolded so fast. I didn't get to the final, but I learnt so much in those two races about how to position myself better at the right time.

One of the things I loved about my first World Championships experience was being part of the squad – the banter, the team talks, the camaraderie with new friends. I wanted to take it all in, to learn as much as I could. The only downer was getting severe food poisoning at the after party, as did some other team members.

When I returned from Athens and Mike Down and I sat down and analysed my performance, we felt like I'd taken a giant stride forward. The experience justified the decision Gav and I had made that I should immerse myself in full-time training and see what happened. And what had happened was that I'd worn a GB vest again with pride after nearly a decade quite literally in the wilderness. I was putting on my running shoes each day with a new perspective. The person who'd suffered stop/start injury setbacks, studied at university, tried not to despair about being unable to run, earnt a degree, worked as a physio, gone travelling and dreamt of reclaiming the teenage promise of Joanne Davis had become Jo Pavey, GB athlete, racing in front of huge crowds against the world's best. I had resolutely refused to let go of my love and passion to run through those lost years, and now I had it back, it felt amazing.

I wanted more of that.

CHAPTER 9

Defying the Doctor

That period from 1996 to 1997 was a seismic shift. Everything had happened so fast, too fast. One minute I was in the pub on Friday nights with my physio mates, getting in a few too many drinks, the next I was smashing my personal bests and qualifying for major championships. I didn't realise at the time – although in hindsight I can see that it was because I'd had a long gap between success as a junior and then this in-at-the-deep-end immersion as an equally naive senior – but I didn't have much of a clue about what to do next. How should I train between seasons? Recover? Achieve balance yet push myself in readiness for 1998? I had never had the luxury of planning a schedule. As a result, being naturally over-enthusiastic, I pushed myself too hard in the winter of 1997 trying to reach the next level.

It was simple inexperience: I'd never had a chance to put together a decent period of solid training. As far as winter training went, I had no point of comparison, but full of enthusiasm I went away to a training camp in Melbourne. Gav and I shared an apartment with friends we'd made in Athens, Andy Hart and his wife Analie, and Mark Sesay, both 800m specialists. We trained hard but had lots of laughs too, and after Mark sadly passed away in 2013 we treasure these memories.

I was excited for the 1998 track season. Things were looking up. It was early summer and the season was about to kick off. With the Athens World Championships experience still fresh in my memory, I was relishing the prospect of a full race schedule. Then disaster struck.

In the middle of a session, I felt an intense pain shoot through my knee and I pulled up. That was it. Game over. Another season to sit out.

It was a bad injury, severe enough, in fact, to need an operation. In September 1998 I underwent surgery, but, disastrously, it caused a lot of damage to my knee and I'm still left with the after-effects now. If I fully straighten my knee, my kneecap locks on the scar tissue and I have to release it by hand. At the time, back on crutches and unable to walk without pain, I had no idea of the scale of the damage. In the early stages, the prognosis was never clear. Doctors and specialists offered conflicting opinions. Three months. Six months. Another three? I went to see another specialist in Leeds a year after the operation as I was still getting so much pain when walking. He told me the only way I'd have any chance of running again was to undergo more surgery, to remove the lump of scar tissue that had been created. He said that if I didn't have more surgery, then I'd never run again. And he meant it.

I declined more surgery. It had already taken me a year to achieve this level of healing and I didn't want to risk going back to square one. My thoughts were completely fixated on battling back with what I had. I had lost trust in the idea of surgery. I'm not suggesting it's not sometimes helpful to sportspeople, as it clearly is, but on a personal level, I had experienced so many recommendations over the years which I had politely declined, not wanting to risk more invasive treatment to my body. The most laughable suggestion was from one surgeon who wanted to re-attach my toe bone in an upside-down position in order to get more mechanical range to help an Achilles injury.

The injury plus the surgery cost me another two and a half years, which is a long time to be unable to pursue the career you love – especially when you're in your twenties and you've already missed six consecutive seasons and don't imagine you'll still be doing this when you turn forty. The constant cycle of optimism and setbacks, rehab, pain and swelling was frustrating, but I didn't get depressed. I have always put life into perspective and have the attitude that I should consider myself fortunate, and I do. It sounds a bit of a cliché, I know, but I believe you should be thankful for your lot in life when you hear of people having terrible illnesses or see awful suffering around the world. I know worse things happen than an injury or a disappointing race.

In September 1999, I turned twenty-six, yet I had still only had one proper injury-free season as a senior athlete. I didn't dwell on it. I did, however, sometimes have to deal with comments that I considered unsupportive from other runners. They were unrelenting in suggesting I should accept that I wouldn't make it back, and that I should just get on with other things. I was hurt by that attitude. Who wants to give up on their dream when they feel like they've only just got started? I still enjoyed going up to Mike's group. I had some good pals there, like Charlie and Lucy with whom I always had a bit of a gossip. I would tell myself I was a month away from full training. Just four more weeks and I'll be back. But unfortunately time went on and on. Even though I was doing as much rehabilitation work and cross-training as I could, I was an athlete who had once again gone off the radar. I treasured my GB kit from Athens but I wasn't a player in the ongoing world of competition. I was back on the outside, wishing I could step in.

I felt isolated at times. Perhaps if I'd been part of an athletics Centre of Excellence, somewhere like Loughborough University where many of Britain's athletes train, it would have been different. I would have been going into the facility every day, and perhaps training alongside other injured athletes in the gym. It would have been favourable to feel part of the group and reap the benefits of a team atmosphere, a bit like the university and hospital camaraderie that I'd thrived on. Nevertheless, I remained focused on getting back to my dream. I couldn't run but when walking became less painful, I took to walking for hours. Gav and I used to drive to beautiful locations at the weekends and walk and talk and the time would run away from us. In the week, rather than drive, I chose to walk an hour and ten minutes to the pool, do my aqua-jog session, and then walk the hour and ten minutes back. Mike, who always supported me, used to comment on how fit I looked with this regime that I'd made up for myself – even though I wasn't running a step.

With the issues I had threatening to end my running career, it was necessary to have flexibility over my time. I needed to be able to cross-train, do rehab and receive the crucial physiotherapy treatment at a clinic which was a long distance away from home in Bristol. I was lucky to be treated by Neil

Black, now performance director of British Athletics and a physiotherapist by training. He was based in Crawley, in West Sussex,
and it could take me up to seven hours to make the round trip
for treatment. That was potentially the whole day taken, so the
only way to make that work was to try to miss both morning and
evening rush hours. That meant leaving at 4.30 a.m. to get an
early appointment with Neil and then driving back to Bristol in
time to call in on the gym where I'd been given free off-peak
membership, pour strong coffee down my throat, and do
whatever training I could. I'd always ensure I got to Crawley
early, leaving leeway for traffic hold-ups, as it would be daft to
drive all that way and miss the appointment. I'd walk around a
twenty-four-hour supermarket if I was stupidly early. It wasn't a
cheery experience. Then I'd have the treatment and leave
buoyed up again by Neil. He was an excellent physio, and
always had a laugh about the new words or phrases I invented
to try to personalise the feedback about my injury. As a physio
myself, I knew the lingo, but it's different when you're trying to
be helpful in conveying exactly what you're experiencing.
'Isolationally dysfunctional' was a phrase I coined for a small part
that isn't working. It was a fun relationship; his encouragement
kept me going.

During that period I was leading a pretty lonely existence:
driving up and down the motorway by myself, then going to the
gym by myself, knowing the odd person to say hello to, but that
was about it. And even that could be perilous. A guy who trained
daily at the gym asked one day if I fancied a coffee. I assumed
he meant a matey coffee comparing injury woes, because I was
wearing a wedding ring and my status was perfectly obvious.
He had other ideas. We were sitting there in the gym coffee bar
in broad daylight when I realised what was on his mind and I

had to make my excuses and leave sharpish. And then avoid him on future trips to the gym . . .

People wondered why I was putting myself through all this. That question took on more resonance one rainy morning on the last stretch of the M25 before joining the M23 for Crawley. In my rear-view mirror I could see a white van speeding up to overtake me. Before I knew it, the van had clipped the corner of my car and sent me in a massive spin. It felt like a Waltzer ride at a funfair. I reacted in sheer panic, turning the wheel to try to regain control, but to no avail. I was convinced that another vehicle would smash into me as I was spinning. The fact that it didn't was miraculous. My car slammed into the central crash barrier, ricocheted back across into the inside lane and ended up pointing towards the central reservation and totally obstructing the lane. A car was coming straight for me. It was only a matter of seconds before I was hit. The young woman at the wheel managed to slow down enough so that the impact didn't do too much damage to either of our cars, but traffic kept pelting past us. We abandoned our vehicles, which were both now blocking the inside lane, and stood on the bank waiting for help, petrified that someone would smash into our wreckage. No one stopped for ages. It was terrifying. Eventually, to our utter relief, a guy in an old Sierra pulled up like a Samaritan. He said he'd turn my car around and leave it on the hard shoulder facing the right direction, and he moved the other girl's car too – and then he drove off. We barely had time to thank him. We were both terribly shaken up. When the police arrived to assess the scene, they gave me the go-ahead to continue my journey. It seemed crazy to carry on to my physio appointment but I was almost there. The spinning across the lanes and the unfolding drama was mentally traumatic, but miraculously there hadn't been much damage. On one level I felt incapable of driving and on another I felt bionic simply to be in one piece.

Gav and I decided that to assist in my return to running it would be helpful to get advice from someone who had been there and done it as an athlete at international level. Chris Boxer kindly agreed to be my mentor, and later became my coach. I knew her by repute as the 1982 1,500m Champion, and I'd met her at the 1997 World Championships in Athens when she was working as the trackside interviewer for the BBC. One day I sat down with Chris and Gav, and discussed starting to run again. I told them my knee felt like it was improving and I thought I could try again. I was playing down my pain, of course, but slowly, during the early spring of 2000, despite the grim prognosis from the specialist, I had sensed my knee was gradually starting to settle down. Slowly and tentatively, I started to get back to running again. At first I ran for just a few minutes around a cricket field, testing it out to see how it would react. For a long while it would always swell a bit after running, and inevitably there were flare-ups and setbacks along the way. I had to monitor it to ensure things were generally going in the right direction. With Chris's help, I rebuilt my training very slowly. Her advice was: 'Don't do what you should do, do what you can do.'

Her sensible approach countered my tendency to be 'over-enthusiastic'. She understood how to balance the need to return to fitness with the importance of not pushing too hard, and risking yet another injury. With Chris's guidance, we broke my training down to basics and started working out what the priorities were. We knew I had to be extremely careful. In fact, throughout 2000 I never ran for more than thirty-five minutes at a time. I was still experiencing a lot of discomfort in my knee and also in my other hip beyond the thirty-to-thirty-five-minute mark. I also ran a very low weekly mileage, peaking at a maximum of 40 miles per week, which is nothing for a middle-distance athlete with ambitions to make the Olympics, but I couldn't entertain what might be considered classic training. I had to train how I could, focusing on good interval sessions and tempo runs (or threshold runs, i.e. – running just under the pace at which your body produces more lactate than it can clear). Coming back from a serious injury, any gain you might get from extra miles is likely to be overturned by potential injury risk, so we concentrated on the crucial sessions – and it wasn't long before we began to see the benefit.

However, it wasn't until April 2000 that I was even ready to gently introduce interval sessions. I started with 2 x 2 minutes, then the following week 3 x 2 minutes and so on until I reached 6 x 2 minutes. Then I was ready to hit the track. We continued to add a rep a week until my sessions were 5 x 1,000m or 6 x 800m. My tempo runs were fifteen minutes long but fast, perhaps not always threshold in the strict scientific sense, more eyeballs out, doing them as hard as I could handle, often nearly being sick when I finished. I had a huge amount of fitness to regain, but this schedule started to move things in the right direction.

Nevertheless, the fact that it was April of an Olympic year, and I'd only just started introducing some specific training after being out for two and a half years, meant getting an Olympic place was a big ask. I'd always been a 1,500m runner, but to add into the mix, it was decided that I should target an event I'd never done before – the 5,000m. Olympic year may not be everyone's ideal choice of timing to switch events, and I certainly felt I had unfinished business with the 1,500m, but there was good reason for this strategy. Going for a longer event could allow me to do more of the specific work for it away from the track, and do more of the sessions on grass to reduce the risk of injury. Given the amount of time I'd had out, this could help prevent further injuries. I also felt that, long term, the longer distances might suit me better. I embarked on putting in efforts around the softer surface of a cricket field, and went to the track relatively infrequently. The track sessions, though, were crucial as races approached to make sure I was hitting my target times, even if there were less of them than I'd ideally do. That important track work, minimal as it was, would make or break my Olympic chances.

Throughout my treatment in 1998 and 1999, another problem had emerged that I had to make sure I managed. As well as the hallux rigidus and the knee, I had unusually poor flexion, or forward bend, in my spine. In fact, I discovered I only had 'normal flexion' at L3 and L4, vertebrae in the lumbar or lower region of my back. The rest of my backbone was pretty knackered, which is not good news for a distance runner. Physio Neil Black and I used to laugh at how ridiculously far I was from being able to touch my toes. I'm like that to this day – it often makes me feel far from athletic! Sciatica has regularly flared up over the years but trying to get more range in my spine always exacerbated the symptoms. We worked out the best way forward was not to try to fix the problem, but to work on preventing it getting worse.

During 2000, as I was dedicating my time to attempting Olympic qualification, it became impossible to consider the regular long days of driving to Neil's physiotherapy clinic. I started seeing Zara Ford in nearby Portishead. Neil discussed my problems with her and she took over my treatment. Zara was great and helped keep me going. She was an expert in osteopathy and physio techniques, and also had specialist knowledge in Pilates. She had a Pilates machine with the full trapeze set-up and we had fun with my complete inability to use it. I was useless! I had to face the fact that even though my bio-mechanical problems might affect the way I run, I had to go with what I've got. Runners of all levels have bio-mechanical issues of a sort – something they feel that if they could change, it would make them a better athlete – but I think it's best to get on with making the best of what you are.

I was pleased with my rate of improvement. Firstly I ran a couple of decent 3,000m races. They did feel tough, though, a bit of a shock to the system, especially as Chris had told me to do them in racing flats rather than spikes to protect my legs. These early races served to boost my fitness, but to qualify for the Olympics I needed to run a decent 5,000m. I had to run the qualifying time and, on top of that, I had to finish in the top two in the British trials. I had never run a 5,000m race. The whole situation was rather daunting but I was also excited by the challenge.

My first target was to get the qualifying time. Leaving it to the trials themselves would have been a massive gamble, having never run the event before. I therefore entered the 5,000m at the Norwich Union meeting at Crystal Palace at the beginning of August, fully aware of what I had to do. All my family were aware of how significant a race this was for me.

As we drove to London I thought Gav seemed unusually quiet. I put it down to nerves, and everything we'd put into this day as a couple. We were at a garage en route to the hotel when Gav received a call from his dad. By the end of the conversation Gav had relief and emotion all over his face. It was only then that he told me that his mum Sheila – who'd had a heart attack in June and was due for a triple bypass operation later in the autumn – had that morning been rushed to hospital for emergency surgery. Unbeknownst to me, Gav had received that news early in the morning just as we were packing up to drive to London and he'd kept it to himself because he didn't want to upset me before the race. I was confused at first about why Gav hadn't told me – we've always shared everything – but he explained, and said she was out of theatre and the procedure had gone well. Sheila had specifically asked Gav's dad Dave not to tell me until we knew she was going to be fine. She said she wanted me to go to the Olympics no matter what the outcome of her op might be. I burst into tears, not only shocked about what had been happening but also relieved that she was going to be all right, and emotional, too, because the family had secretly and thoughtfully agreed to keep it from me that morning. They thought if I had known of the emergency, I wouldn't have been able to run with the stress and worry. We had a big hug. The day was always going to be tough mentally, and this added an enormous emotional impact.

I now had even more reason to ensure I ran well. The gun sounded. I settled into my rhythm, the lap times of the Olympic qualifying goal etched in my mind. I set about maintaining my focus, trying not to tense up as I methodically ticked off each lap time. Some of the world's best athletes were in the race. It was such a high-class field, I had to suppress my schoolgirl instinct of just racing hard, going with that freedom of running whereby I simply ignored the clock. Trying to run with the front-runners at my level of fitness and with no previous experience of the event wouldn't have been very sensible. I had a job to do: to get my time. Once that was done I would be 'allowed' to race. 'Don't take any chances,' Chris had said. 'Just do what you need to do.' I finished well down the field, but it was the time that mattered: 15:18.51 – nearly 17 seconds inside the Olympic qualifying time! Chris, Gav and I were thrilled. I was pleased to be able to share the news with our families, particularly Gav's mum.

I had one tentative foot in the Sydney Olympics. But the task was by no means complete. I now had to finish in the top two in the trial to achieve automatic selection for the Games. The AAA National Championships and Olympic trials were held in Birmingham. I was up against Paula Radcliffe, who had been a World Championships silver medallist over 10,000m the previous year, and she was in fantastic form. I knew all I needed to do was finish second. Again Chris said, 'Don't take any chances. Race, but race this only to make sure you get that automatic spot. You must not risk that second place.' I was in 'job to do' mode, knowing what needed to be done.

Paula finished first, but when I crossed the line in second place in a time of 15 minutes 21.15 seconds I was overwhelmed. It was the happiest second place of my career. That was it. I'd made it! I was going to an Olympic Games! If I never did anything in running ever again, I'd made the GB Olympic team. My dream had come true. It was an unbelievable feeling. The level of competition in Sydney the following month would unquestionably be tough, but I knew that I would give it my all without compromise. It felt quite emotional to be able to say the words I'd thought might be a silly dream since I was a child: 'I'm going to run in an Olympic Games!'

Gav and I were so thrilled. One of the first people we phoned was our old coach Tony. He had been there at the start of my career and helped show me that distance running was where my talent lay; now I was going to an Olympics! Tony was obviously delighted, and Gav and I headed to the pub to celebrate with Chris and my family, and later went out for a curry with my brother Matt and his wife Lorna to mark the moment.

Just a day or so before the flight to Australia, I had one more race: a 3,000m at the Gateshead Norwich Union Classic. I recall there was a light drizzle, and, up against Paula Radcliffe and Sonia O'Sullivan, I certainly wasn't expecting to figure in the placings. I was still emerging from years of injury. Chris was talking about me running 8:45 or so. Sonia, the European 5,000m and 10,000m gold medallist and world cross-country champion, was in terrific form and put in her trademark kick sprint at the end, leaving us all for dead with a time of 8:33 or something. Libby Hickman of the United States followed in second place, running 8:35, then behind her was Paula in 8:36, and then me, also claiming an 8:36. Chris and Gav were elated. This was such a huge step forward for me – a major breakthrough. If I could go sub 8:40 at 3,000m, I should be able to get close to sub 15:00 at 5,000m. With this race under my belt, I could head off to the training camp in Australia, and to the Olympics, feeling a little more ready.

Me with my mum and dad in 1975.

An early primary school photo.

With my brothers Matt and Jon.

Some of my earliest races, running for Devon in 1988. At the time I couldn't imagine running in top level senior competitions.

With Gav and Tony White, my coach at Exeter Harriers who did so much to encourage me as a youngster.

On our trip around France in our Ford Fiesta in 1993 – it was mad but a lot of fun.

Our wedding day in 1995.

Enjoying some fun times in Bristol with my physio friends Dana, Ross, Kol and Mel.

Enjoying the views in Queenstown, New Zealand
on our backpacking trip.

Surveying the damage in Fiji after
Cyclone Gavin. The locals joked
about this English chap who'd
brought his own cyclone, but the
devastation was terrible.

After a tough training session in
New Zealand, a very refreshing dip
in one of the beautiful lakes.

Running in the 1,500m national trials in 1997 in Birmingham. I was so thrilled to qualify for my first international champs and see that my dream wasn't that crazy after all.

Getting ready to line up at my international debut in the World Championships in Athens in 1997.

Enjoying the atmosphere with fellow GB athletes Rob Hough, Andy Hart, Paula Radcliffe and Diane Allagreen.

Very excited to be off to my first Olympic Games in Sydney in 2000!

I was thrilled and amazed to finish my first Olympic race in a personal best and qualify for the 5,000m final.

I could hardly believe that just a few years earlier I was peering through the fence as they built the Olympic Stadium, daring to dream I could one day race there.

Pushing hard in the 5,000m in the 2004 Olympic Games in Athens – probably the only time I'll start a race on one day and finish it on another!

On my way to silver in the 5,000m – my first outdoor major track championship medal – in the 2006 Commonwealth Games in Melbourne.

Showing our medals; being on the podium is such a special moment.

The iconic view of Tower Bridge during the London marathon when I ran it in 2011. The atmosphere of big races like this is so amazing and I love seeing all the kids with their homemade banners supporting their parents.

I was really happy to do more road racing that year, such as the Bupa London 10,000.

I was asked to recreate the famous photo of Sebastian Coe running in Richmond Park, where I did lots of my training while we lived in Teddington.

CHAPTER 10

My First Olympics

Going to my first Olympics was a defining moment in my career. And it seems ridiculous, even to me, that I've now been to four of them. Competing at an Olympic Games feels like you've achieved a major lifetime goal as an athlete. I remembered the time when my friend Andy Hart was selected for his first World Championships and was so chuffed, and Fatima Whitbread asked him on live TV how he thought he'd do: 'I don't know,' he replied. 'I'm just going for the kit!' He didn't mean that literally; the line just popped out. It was said with a mix of incredulity and excitement that I could now fully understand. Only one person in each event is going to win the gold medal, but we are all so proud to put on our country's vest and perform to the best of our ability to make our nation proud.

When I packed to travel out to Australia, I was heading to only my third ever race over 5,000m at only my second senior major championships. What made the journey particularly special was the thought that I was returning to the place where, three years earlier, Gav and I had peered through the fence at the stadium foundations as backpackers, daring to dream that I could get myself fit enough to try to qualify. It felt surreal that I was now going to be on the other side of that fence in the stadium in Homebush – that I was going to experience performing there as an insider. To add to the feeling that it was 'meant to be', the GB holding camp was held in Surfers Paradise, where Gav and I had toasted New Year's Eve, up to our waists in foam as a Nirvana tribute band played to the crowds. This time, however, we couldn't get up to such exploits. We were there with a purpose: to prepare for our events within a focused team environment, protected from any distractions. Inside the camp, the excitement built up day by day, and the camaraderie was fantastic. I soon settled in but poor Gav had to find an alternative place to stay.

At that stage, he wasn't my coach – although, as well as being my husband, he was also my training partner, pacer and support system – but he wasn't part of the GB team and therefore entitled to official travel and accommodation. In the early summer of 2000, he and I had purchased a house in Bristol, trying to do the responsible thing, which had swallowed up nearly all our savings. We weren't skint, but the mortgage deposit and outgoings challenged our cash flow, which meant Gav had a very tight budget to stick to in order to accompany me to Sydney. His flight took a large chunk of the budget, but we calculated enough for accommodation. When we arrived, however, we realised that not all of the training venues were suitable for me. My knee couldn't handle any undulations or inclines; ideally, I needed good flat grass. Having been so injury-prone, we didn't want to risk anything by having to train under less-than-ideal circumstances. As I couldn't expect to be given transport at all times to wherever I'd have to go to train, we decided to hire a car. The problem was that Gav now had hardly any money left for his accommodation and so, on several nights, he ended up kipping in the car! On another occasion, he found a cheap motel room only to discover that it was next door to a brothel. It was not exactly the glamorous Olympic lifestyle you might imagine. I shared a room with Kelly and, as usual, we had lots of laughs. I tried my hardest to be tidy with my stuff in the room, but this is a big ask for me. Compared to Kel, who is immaculately tidy, I never came close. She would often laugh at my recurring problem: an inability to find anything.

The training went well. Apart from the times I went to the track, I did all my training around the flat Pizzey Park. Other athletes used Pooh Park, which was a bit hillier. The names of the venues provided a source of amusement. Gav kept extremely busy, pacemaking the other athletes for parts of their sessions when he wasn't training with me. He had no official team role, but he did this until he completely injured his calf and could no longer run!

Soon the big day dawned, the day the Olympic Flame would arrive in the stadium to signal the start of the Games. The athletics didn't begin until the second week and so we wouldn't move into the Olympic Village until three or four days before our competition. As a result, we weren't part of the Opening Ceremony, but watched it live from the holding camp on a huge TV screen. They laid on a barbecue and a local primary school came to the camp with a group of sweet little children to put on a special parade for us, and there was also Aboriginal dancing and music with didgeridoos – one of several touches that helped us fully celebrate the experience.

I couldn't wait to get out on the track to compete in my first Games. I was living in the moment and loving it. The experience became even more overwhelming when we moved down to the Athletes' Village. My brother Matt had kindly given us £250 towards our Olympic trip, which Gav used to invest in a video camera during the flight stopover in Hong Kong. I made endless videos just walking around the village, revelling in its extraordinary atmosphere. It was buzzing with nerves and excitement.

The village is a little town in its own right with a population made up purely of athletes and coaches, the medical teams and other backroom staff crucial to each national squad. Again, I shared with Kelly. At first we were allocated a room so tiny it did not accommodate our luggage! We were then given the option of staying in a Portakabin in the back garden. We moved into it, embracing the sense of adventure. I was taken with the colour and vibrancy of the village. The balconies of the accommodation buildings were draped with the flags of whatever nation was housed there and everyone walked around in their national kit. In Sydney, the whole village seemed particularly enormous because the buildings were low-rise and there were some nice big grassy areas, which meant it covered a vast, sprawling site. It was so big that the team had a couple of golf buggies to whizz athletes around to spare our legs. Designed as a self-sufficient town, it had its own bus system, gyms, cinemas, arcades of shops and food. Oh, the food! There were more than 10,000 athletes at the 2000 Olympic Games – a massive number to cater for, so you might think the quality would suffer – but the food was amazing, with so much choice, catering for the tastes of the whole world. Everything was free, with plenty of healthy food on offer – but also a free McDonald's and fridges stocked with Magnum ice creams. I had to be extremely self-controlled and resist the kid-in-the-sweet-shop temptation to go for it, at least until after my race!

Gav and I had very much shared our build-up to the Sydney

Games with our good friends Andy and Analie Hart. We met up so regularly we felt like a team of four. At the trials when I qualified, the job somehow hadn't felt totally complete until Andy had also qualified for the 800m. As the competitors, Andy and I had the same routine while Gav and Analie shared similar supportive roles. In Sydney, we used to joke we'd done an innocent wife swap: Andy and I often hanging out together in the Athletes' Village, and Gav and Analie hanging out together outside it.

Once in the village, time whizzed by and soon the day arrived when I would compete in my first ever Olympics. As well as the excitement, I had such nerves. Simply to be there in that atmosphere in the Olympic Stadium was an unbelievable experience, let alone running in front of 110,000 people screaming louder than you think possible. Fortunately, the 5,000m heat was scheduled on the first night of the athletics so I didn't have to wait around for days while everyone else's events were under way. Once I'd readjusted to the glare of the stadium floodlights and taken in the incredible surroundings, I took a moment to look up at the Olympic Flame burning from the huge, elevated cauldron. It was a stirring sight: here I was, competing in the Olympics, knowing I was only here because I had somehow kept alive my own burning passion to run. To be there was such a joy compared to a normal meeting; I knew I would instinctively give every ounce of effort to try to get through to the final. When I toed the line for the start of my heat, I allowed myself a brief reflection on that moment when Gav and I had gazed through the wire fence surrounding a large hole in the ground and huge heaps of earth spoils excavated during construction of the stadium's foundations. That private moment of contemplation, taking stock of how much we'd gone through to get me here, both relaxed and fired me up.

I can't remember much of my qualifying heat lap by lap. My nerves were considerable but I channelled them to my advantage. I've never used a sports psychologist, even though I appreciate how helpful they can be to some athletes. Somehow I've always been able to get into the zone. It's a sort of heightened state, fuelled by the extra adrenalin, which is hard to describe beyond the fact that it genuinely does lift my performance. It's about not dreading the pain I know I am about to suffer but to turn it around and relish the challenge. When the pain bites, it's a case of 'Come on, enjoy the pain' because every step is getting me nearer my goal. Over the distance, I'm concentrating on being economical. If I tense up, I lose energy. I'm aware of my thought processes, but they are almost subconscious. When a race goes well, my body seems to take control instinctively. I also believe that you shouldn't set limits on yourself. This was the Olympics, and however unrealistic it might have seemed, I was going to do my utmost to make that final.

To my absolute delight, I crossed the line in a personal best of 15:08.82, to finish second behind Sonia O'Sullivan and one place ahead of the reigning 10,000m World Champion Gete Wami of Ethiopia. Three 5,000m heats had been held to whittle the field of fifty down to fifteen finalists and I would be one of them. I'd made the final of an Olympic Games! Chris, my coach, was working for the BBC as a trackside interviewer so I was able to thank her both in person and live on air for helping me to become an Olympian. I couldn't wait to get off the track to hug Gav. We were so overjoyed. I remember lying in bed that night thinking, 'Wow. I'm in an Olympic final.' At the beginning of the year I'd been forever stuck in slow traffic on the motorway, travelling to and from physio, or sitting in the gym doing core work watching people run on treadmills, wishing I was fit enough to do the same. And now I was going to line up alongside the best in the world.

I had three days to recover after my heat. My muscles were so sore the next morning I was barely able to walk. It wasn't lack of fitness. Rather a lack of track adaptation. My performance in the qualifying heat had taken its toll. I was simply not used to running flat out on a hard surface for such a relatively long time in spikes. My legs stiffened and rebelled in protest. We knew this could happen. But after such a long time away injured I couldn't justify doing any more track work than I had done. If I could, I would have incorporated more track work to condition my muscles so that I would have recovered more quickly and been in a better state for the final. I'm not making excuses; nor do I have regrets. I had trained the way I had to in order to reach the Olympics. I knew it would be tough with my lack of experience and the lack of miles in my legs, but if I *had* done more track work, I may have broken down again with injuries, so that was simply the way it had to be.

On the night of the final, the stadium was packed to the rafters with passionate spectators. I later learnt the figure was 112,524, a new record attendance at an Olympic Games, and they created the most incredible atmosphere to compete in. It was the night the host nation's poster girl Cathy Freeman won the 400m. So for the home crowd, this was *the* night of the Games. I went through my warm-up: fifteen minutes of gentle jogging, stretches to warm up all the muscle groups, drills to activate those muscles. We were summoned to the call room for about forty minutes, and that's always a tense time: waiting with all your rivals, some sitting still, others hyperactive. I'm usually worried about when to fit in the last opportunity to use the toilet. And I tend to play with my shoelaces. I want them to be absolutely perfect: imagine having to run all those laps in an Olympic race with your shoelaces too tight or too loose! I do struggle with knowing when to stop re-doing them. My nerves matched the huge occasion. One comical thing happened as we were led from the call room through a long tunnel that led up to the stadium. Normally you walk calmly to the track, but this time, for some reason, everyone – athletes and officials – broke into a run as if we were a football team coming on to the pitch! And then we all looked at each other in bewilderment. Why had we done that?

It was reassuring to see the friendly – and equally puzzled – face of Sonia O'Sullivan in the mix in there. Everything about the process of racing seemed on a different level that night. We were led out towards the start, then held back by the official for a minute near the triple jump pit so their competition could continue. I had the most fantastic view of Jonathan Edwards's winning jump. An amazing moment.

I stood on the start line, again conscious of that Olympic Flame, looking up at it and feeling its symbolism. I had run my first ever 5,000m at the start of August and now, just seven weeks later, I was in an Olympic final. Of course it felt surreal, a bit like something you might daydream about as a kid, knowing it's nothing but an illusion in your mind.

'Stand up! Stand up!' the starter was shouting.

He wasn't happy with something – someone had a toe over the line, maybe, or there was a distraction from a field event. I took a deep breath. Waited. Then bang! We were off. My legs felt awful right away. But I just went for it, running to the death, giving it my all. I stayed with the pace for as many laps as I could. It felt tough. With five laps to go I was still in touch, in tenth place, but as the leaders upped the pace I started to slip back. I gave it my all and finished twelfth – in 14 minutes and 58.27 seconds. The Romanian Gabriela Szabo won and Sonia O'Sullivan took silver. Despite coming in behind the breakaway leading pack, I'd gone under the 15-minute mark for the first time and improved my personal best by 10 seconds. That was a huge boost and gave me hope for the future.

After my final, I didn't want the Olympic experience to end. I was determined to soak up every last wonderful moment. It was like that glorious end-of-term feeling you have as a child, with a long holiday stretching out ahead of you and nothing to do but have fun. And of course I didn't want to miss the Closing Ceremony. So Gav and I arranged to stay on and we really made the most of our freedom: I no longer had to resist the lure of those free chocolate caramel Magnums and we went out all the time, having a blast. We watched all the athletics we could, and then went partying in Sydney until the early hours. Because my event featured early on in the competition schedule, some of the other athletes in my house still hadn't finished competing. So sometimes I'd creep back in to the team accommodation. There is no way I'd risk waking up my teammates. I certainly couldn't risk the noise that going out into the back garden to the Portakabin would make! So I'd lie on the floor fully clothed so as to avoid disturbing the others. One random night there was no need for accommodation. Somehow, we ended up getting a lift in the car of parents who'd just picked up their kids from a graduation party. We sat in the back, with the kids. To this day we're not sure how we ended up in this situation, but it was their idea to drop us off at an Irish bar that stayed open until the early hours. We eventually got back on a morning train, packed with commuters on their way to work. On the train we met 1,500m runner John Mayock who had also enjoyed a good night.

In retrospect, this period was probably the longest stretch of 'freedom from training' I've ever had after a Games. I really went into celebratory mode after running in my first Olympics, but in the years to come my priority was to stay in good shape. For distance runners, the autumn is an important time and I would switch my focus to events such as the Great North Run and the Great South Run. But after 2000, the only plan was to start winter training after a decent rest, and in sunny Australia, that point seemed a long time away. We stayed for the Closing Ceremony and I was able to walk around the track for a final time, reflecting on this incredible experience. Ticker tape fell everywhere as part of the parade. Many athletes tried to catch it, to keep as a memento. It's nice to have a tangible reminder to go with all the wonderful memories.

Our mate Andy retired soon after Sydney. To this day, he runs an 800m on the anniversary of the day he competed in the Olympics – not to be competitive, just for a bit of fun, so he can measure how much slower he gets over time. On one of these anniversary runs, he managed to fall over on the track as he struggled to take off his kit – and broke his arm. He was so determined to continue his tradition he ran his 800m anyway, thankful, I suppose, he wasn't a 10,000m runner.

I arrived back from Sydney brimming with plans about how to approach the future. But before we sat at the kitchen table, focusing on working out the strategy for 2001, there was a final occasion of post-Olympic partying to enjoy. The entire British athletics squad was invited to Buckingham Palace, just the team in a room at a proper Palace function. Unfortunately, Gav couldn't go in because he wasn't an official member of the squad, but he kindly volunteered to drive me and my friend Marian Sutton, the marathon runner, up to the Palace. The Palace staff were discreetly generous with the wine. Very generous, in fact. My glass always seemed to be full. Every time I turned around to talk to someone, it must have been refilled. When the Queen arrived, we formed a line and she came down, kindly taking time to speak to some of us. My friends Andy and Marian were standing on either side of me, propping me up, hoping for dear life that the Queen would not talk to me. I suddenly found myself searching for something to say. 'What a lovely house you've got!' I calmly and politely said to the Queen. I didn't hear the end of that from some of the other members of the team!

CHAPTER 11

Controversy in Canada

Up to 2000, I had a reputation for being one of the most injury-prone athletes you could ever meet, but the Sydney Games proved a watershed. Over the next eight years, I would be considered one of the most consistent. From 2000 to 2008 I attended all of the major outdoor championships – the Commonwealth Games, European Championships, World Championships and Olympic Games – and reached the final at each.

Before Sydney I had only been running about 35 to 40 miles a week but over the winter of 2000 and spring of 2001 I was slowly and steadily able to build up my mileage and the intensity of my training sessions. Of course, there were setbacks. The truth was, I had spent the whole of 2000 injured or in pain to some degree. First my knee, and then a hip issue. But I had never seen injury as a reason to stop. Every time I did a run at the camp on the Gold Coast, I was in pain and felt my progress was being limited. After the Olympics, the pain in my hip hadn't eased so I went to see Gerard Hartmann, who ran a sports injury clinic in Limerick and treated athletes like Kelly, Paula Radcliffe, the Kenyans, Marian Sutton, Elaine Fitzgerald and many others who had all sought his help. It was quite an experience; Gerard believes in getting really deep into the tissue to sort out the problem. I'd hear squeals from his treatment room above the soothing background music of 'Morning Has Broken'. But it was a very good programme. He set me specific exercises to do twice a day, for between 60 and 90 minutes, as well as treatment to correct and strengthen my body mechanics, and I was able to resume training.

In January 2001, we flew out to Johannesburg to reap the benefit of training in a warm climate. Stepping off the plane, I recall feeling pleasantly shocked by the South African heat. I love running in the heat and I feel like it really boosts my fitness. Many runners woke up early to avoid the hottest part of the day. When I stayed in accommodation with other athletes they often though it was funny that I was heading out so late in the morning. This was my first experience on the continent, but the university city of Potchefstroom was where a lot of my team-mates based themselves in the winter, such as Kelly Holmes, Helen Clitheroe, Mo Farah, Anthony Whiteman, Andy Graffin, Chris Thompson and Sam Haughian. Situated on the banks of a river about 75 miles south-west of Johannesburg, Potchefstroom offered a great environment conducive for warm-weather train-ing and an immaculate grass athletics track, as well as the oppor-tunity to run from your front door and enjoy the camaraderie of a dedicated athletics community. We often met up for coffee at the Die Akker café, which served great cream teas – complete with freshly baked scones, clotted cream, jam and a pile of biltong. The dried, cured meat is a national tradition, but I never warmed to it as an appropriate accompaniment to a cream tea. Gav used to scoff mine.

I was there to focus on my running, although I also wanted to learn more about the country. We made a point of visiting

Robben Island where Nelson Mandela was imprisoned, which I found humbling, as well as visiting game parks and Simon's Town where we swam with penguins. South Africa is a land of paradoxes, which are difficult to reconcile, but the beauty of the landscape gets under your skin. At just over 4,000 feet above sea level, the city of Potchefstroom and its surroundings didn't have particularly high altitude, but it was great for building up my mileage. With potentially loads of different places to run with ideal surfaces underfoot, it made a perfect training base, especially as I was in year one of our five-year plan to build up my weekly total to 100 miles by 2005. I did most of my miles along the railway trail, a dirt road that went along the side of the track all the way to Johannesburg. It was roasting hot with no shade but the surface was perfect for running and I liked it as an 'out and back' route. Sunburn was a hazard; it was easy to get burnt as I ran facing the sun all the way out then had the sun on my back all the way home. I have many memories of sun cream stinging my eyes. Very, very long and slow trains would often pass with the drivers waving at me and tooting their horns. On one occasion a man heard me approaching from behind and pulled a knife. He immediately apologised and explained he thought I was going to attack him.

With diligent care of my knee and hip, I had started to get a decent block of training in, but just before returning to the UK, I was gutted to sustain a shin injury. I returned to Gerard Hartmann's clinic to get it sorted. I missed the start of the 2001 season, but had to start racing in July if I had any chance of making the championships. I raced a 3,000m in Lausanne in July. I finished seventh in 8:58.20 – a disappointing result. Eleven days later, I ran in the AAA British Championships in Birmingham and won the 5,000m, which meant I had earnt selection for the World Championships in Edmonton, Canada, the following month.

Gav was now acting as my coach. Chris Boxer had moved to Scotland so throughout 2001 we were trying to decide the best way forward. Gav wasn't too sure whether to take over the coaching role at first. We had been pleased with the way things had worked out while we were backpacking in the winter of 1996/7. Then, it was just us on our own, setting the training together. Continuity in approach was our priority. We were concerned that someone else may not understand how extremely prone to injury I was and allow the flexibility I needed with my training. We decided to go ahead with Gav becoming my coach. Former athlete and commentator Tim Hutchings kindly gave us some initial advice and Gav knew he could also get on the blower to Alan Storey, Head of Endurance for UK Athletics, and use him as a sounding board. 'That's bollocks, Gavin!' Alan would say, or 'That's great, I love that!'

The World Championships in Edmonton was a difficult experience for many reasons. I had worked hard to get over my injury problems, and trained as hard as I could around them, but my fitness wasn't at the level it should have been. We arrived in Canada quite a few days before the competition to prepare a plan, which proved just as well because as soon as we landed I developed a strange kidney infection. My legs swelled up, my quads felt like they were splitting; I felt dizzy and I couldn't see clearly. However much fluid I drank, my urine remained dark. It was very mysterious. On the recommendation of Gerard Hartmann, I went to the supermarket and bought litres of pure, unsweetened cranberry juice. Luckily Canada is the second largest cranberry producer in the world and I drank as much as

I could get down me. Eventually my body started functioning properly again. I was rooming with Kelly Holmes again, and when I arrived early and discovered our room faced a busy railway line, I messaged Kelly and warned her it was impossible to sleep with the noise. Being an important member of the GB team, she managed to get us moved before she'd even seen the room. There were two days of torrential rain preceding the championships and on one occasion Kelly persuaded the bus driver to detour right up to the gym door so she could dash in without ruining her hair!

Beyond my little bubble of trying to get myself fit to race, a media storm was brewing. Sadly, doping in athletics became a prime topic of conversation in 2015 but, back in 2001, the championships in Edmonton opened my eyes to this awful side to the sport. Obviously I'd heard of scandals like East Germany's athletics programme and Ben Johnson, but now the focus of world attention at this championship involved an athlete in my race: Olga Yegorova of Russia who had tested positive for the blood booster erythropoietin (EPO) at the Paris Golden League earlier that summer. EPO – a hormone that is produced naturally by the kidneys, but can be produced synthetically – prompts the production of red blood cells. When a cheat injects EPO, more red blood cells are produced and the result is that they can run faster and will tire at a later point than they would naturally because they have more oxygen being delivered to their muscles.

The International Association of Athletics Federations (IAAF) reinstated Yegorova and allowed her to run in Edmonton because of a technicality. The French laboratory tested her urine, but there was no accompanying blood test. This did not mean that EPO was not detected in the urine sample but only that proper testing protocol had not been followed by the authorities. I felt extremely angry about the situation and let down by the inadequacies of drug testing in my sport.

In 2001 I wasn't in prime shape or at the stage in my career to challenge for the medals, but I still found it upsetting. In later years I felt the impact of the inadequacies in drug testing even more personally – because I was getting close to the medals and I was kept off the podium as a result of cheats.

But back to Edmonton . . . It was a disheartening experience. I was appalled to be on the start line of the final with an athlete who'd had EPO detected in her system. I felt she had no right to be there. My heart went out to my good friend Kathy Butler who just missed the cut for the final. The fastest of the non-qualifiers, she'd been deprived of a place in a World Championships final. It wasn't just fellow athletes in Edmonton who were horrified, sports fans following athletics were dismayed too. The atmosphere in the stadium reflected our feelings and frustrations as the crowd booed Yegorova. It was weird to be led out onto the track for a huge event to such a negative reception, and yet the boos were directed at one athlete only. As we raced the crowds continued to boo her and they were still booing long after the race too. It was a media circus with an intense spotlight on us for all the wrong reasons. In 2008, the cheating finally caught up with Yegorova and she was banned, along with six other female Russian athletes. This was after shockingly tampering with the samples, as discovered when the DNA didn't match. We now know that the incident in 2001 was an early sign and the tip of a very big iceberg, beneath which lay a huge problem in Russia that would go unexposed until 2015. This is also indicative of the failings of anti-doping authorities to detect doping in athletics over a lengthy period of time.

The Edmonton final was a tough race on so many levels. I was in Canada knowing my preparation for the event was far from ideal. I finished very disappointingly down in eleventh place. Considering my injury and illness problems, it was to be expected realistically. I often hope I can still pull something out of the bag on the day, but you do need both fitness and determination. I had given it my all in the race. I came away with that in mind, but with some dismay that all was not rosy in my sport. But I would just have to crack on with my training and racing. I would focus on what I could control, and train as hard as I could to try to improve my own performances.

CHAPTER 12

Always Fifth

Another thing that came to light in 2001 for me was a medical condition related to an endocrinology problem. Most runners slow down at the end of races due to muscle fatigue and an accumulation of lactate, but I had to contend with another – very different – issue that caused me to slow down. Over the latter stages of a race I often experienced dizziness: the track would start to sway from side to side and I would feel myself begin to weaken. During the many years of my career where dipsticks were still used for urine testing, I was often told that the sugar level in my urine was at the highest reading and it was suggested that I could be diabetic. I went to the doctor to get this checked out. I also got a kit normally used for diabetics to monitor blood sugar and began to note down the value whenever I could after races and hard sessions. It quickly became apparent that the rise in my blood sugar level wasn't due to the duration of an effort but rather to the intensity, as it would happen in a 1,500m or 5,000m race and later in half marathons. No matter what distance I was racing, my blood sugar level rose suddenly in the closing stages when I was putting in the final kick. The medical team also did some testing on me whilst I was on a GB training camp in South Africa and were surprised at the high levels of sugar in my blood following training sessions. Annoyingly, the sugar stays in my bloodstream rather than being delivered effectively to my muscles. This contributes to the heaviness in my legs and leaves me feeling quite spaced out, dizzy and lacking in energy. After seeing an endocrinologist, it was confirmed that I wasn't diabetic but that I had something like a diabetic response to exercise. He said it was extremely unusual and it would be difficult to do anything about it. I was told to keep an eye on it and report it to the team doctors.

Fortunately, it was not considered a significant long-term health issue but it was deemed to be a potential serious problem during intense exercise. It was also frustrating because it made it much more of a challenge to put in a strong push to finish races. I experimented with my diet, trying to have more pre-race protein and that helped a bit. However, in theory, the main thing I could do would be to get my fitness to a level whereby my body would feel under less stress during the closing stages of a race. Easier said than done! So here I was: a runner with a back that only flexes properly at L3/L4, the toe condition hallux rigidus, a leg that locks when straightened, and now a hyperglycaemia problem too. And that's just for starters – I was crocked, and I was only in my early thirties.

The next few years were enormously exasperating for me. I'd had some good performances, lowered some personal bests, but things seemed to go wrong just at the worst time, and I kept missing out. In 2002 I finished fifth in the European Championships, and fifth in the Commonwealth Games. It felt bitterly disappointing – I was always reaching the finals of the major events, but never realising what I felt was my potential. I seemed to be beached in fifth position on the results table.

I was happy, though, to be working steadily within our
long-term plan and with Gav as my full-time official coach.
Being my husband, he could hardly be part time! In 2003 we
moved from Bristol to Teddington. When my commercial agent
Geoff Wightman retired after the Sydney Games, Gav and I
had gone to a meeting with Kim McDonald in Teddington prior
to joining his agency in late 2000. A former long-distance track
athlete himself, he had gone on to manage athletes such as
Steve Ovett, Sonia O'Sullivan and Peter Elliott, and was well
known for developing the Kenyan runners. Sadly Kim died a
year later – I remember getting the call in Bristol and it was a
devastating shock. It was so hard to believe. He was only
forty-five. When we first met him at his office, we didn't know
that part of London at all. As the meeting came to an end, we
asked Kim if there was anywhere we could go for a run. Any bit
of grass? Very straightforwardly, he gave us directions to walk
back up the high street, turn left and go through a gate. We followed his advice, expecting maybe a couple of football pitches,
but found ourselves at the entrance of the vast, 1,110-acre
Bushy Park, the second largest of London's Royal Parks. We
could certainly see why the area attracted so many runners. By
early 2003, we had moved to Teddington like so many distance
athletes – training in Bushy and Richmond Parks, discovering
the Thames towpath, going out for coffee in the nice cafés,
popping into Tesco on the way home with groceries for supper
before the evening session. We also enjoyed going for a curry
in the evening at Bilas Tandoori, a favourite amongst athletes.
For track sessions, we were close to Tartan tracks in Kingston
and in Walton-on-Thames. Later, a Tartan track was laid down at
St Mary's College near Teddington, which made the location
even more ideal. St Mary's was also home to the UK Athletics

Endurance Centre, where we had access to physios and physiologists like Andy Jones and Charlie Pedlar. It was a great routine and we were close to Heathrow, which made travel to and from races and South African winter camps so much easier. The management agency provided transport so we never even had to worry about organising that. We focused on training and enjoyed a social life with fellow runners Kathy Butler and her husband Andrew, and Benita Willis. Running in Bushy Park, Gav and I would often come across another athlete and we'd join up for a run if we weren't doing a specific session, and routinely meet for coffee.

In 2003, with an eye on running the 5,000m in Athens at the Olympics in the following year, Gav introduced a different approach. I would train for 5,000m – i.e. do high-volume sessions and speed endurance work with lots of 800m and 1,000m reps – but race over 1,500m. Gav felt the races over three and three-quarter laps would allow me to work on my speed whilst gaining valuable tactical experience. It was an interesting approach, and it led to a very pleasing 4:01.79 time in the 1,500m and an 8:37.89 in the 3,000m on the same weekend in early September. This was at the World Athletic Final in Monaco, which meant a proper race with no pacemakers. (A pacemaker is given specific instructions for lap times by the race organisers to ensure a fast race.) I much prefer free races to paced races.

The 1,500m time did make me half wish that I could have a proper go at the 1,500m one year and go sub 4 minutes. After some discussion, however, we felt that the 5,000m was the best option going forward because I didn't have the pure top-end finishing speed of a top 1,500m runner. It was all about championship running and to this day 14:39 at 5,000m is my best PB when compared to 4:01 at 1,500m and so this was the right decision for me.

In early summer 2004 I was in good shape. I'd had a great winter's training in Portugal – three short trips to prepare for the indoor racing season, focusing on the different style of racing and surface – and they'd gone well. I felt the rewards of that hard work when it all came together in a 3,000m race in February in Birmingham in which I broke the British record. In the later laps I had gone to the front and tried to run away from the Ethiopians, Meseret Defar and Tirunesh Dibaba. They tucked in behind and went past me on the final lap. I think they both ran about 8:33 and I was right behind in 8:34. I loved this race. The atmosphere was awesome. Each race that season whetted my appetite for the Olympics in Athens. Having focused on the 1,500m in 2003, I needed a 5,000m qualifying time for the Games.

In May we headed to the Holland Thales FBK Games in Hengelo. I felt good, running freely, enjoying the race when, with about five laps to go, my calf started to feel sore. Two laps to go, I felt the muscle tear. It was unbelievably painful but thanks to the adrenalin flow – and the fact I was running well under the qualifying time – I somehow kept going. I had to make a very quick decision. I could sense the injury was bad, and if I stopped now and didn't get the Olympic qualifying time, I knew I'd never recover soon enough to re-attempt it in time for selection. If I pulled up, I would not be going to the Olympics. So I carried on, aware that I would get my qualifying time, but might well be too injured to compete in the Olympics. It was a dilemma and I had to reason it out swiftly whilst racing. I dropped back behind the field a bit but, decision made, suddenly started working my way back through the field. I was running through excruciating pain but I thought I've just got to go for it and gamble that the muscle would recover in time. I pushed on and finished 2nd in 14:55.04. I'd got the time I needed but at what cost?

The tear was so bad I couldn't even walk. For two months, it was back to that all-too-familiar routine – cross-training twice a day, every day in the pool. Aqua jogging is a good form of cross-training but, because you are not bearing any weight, it's hard to get your heart rate high enough to achieve effective cardiovascular work. It means you have to train much longer in the pool, and much more intensely, to get a similar benefit to running on land. Every day I'd be in the pool for an hour in the morning and an hour in the afternoon. I was fortunate to receive funding for accommodation so Gav and I could be based for six weeks at the High Performance Centre in Birmingham. It was a motivating environment and I received great treatment from physio Dean Kenneally. The Royal Ballet School in Birmingham had kindly let me use their pool for training. I was aqua jogging, swimming and cycling on the stationary bike. I was also obsessively determined to keep some impact going through my bones and muscles to minimise the loss of conditioning. I believed this would be crucial in order to make competing in the Olympics a possibility. There were lots of cricket fields, so even when I couldn't run a step, I developed a galloping motion, with high knee steps, mostly leading with my good leg because I couldn't toe off. I must have looked completely mad! I would also jump up and down on the spot with my ankles in a locked position, because I couldn't propel forwards. People may have thought I was crazy but I believe you've got to do what you can do at all times. My view was that if I waited for my body to be perfect and free of injuries, I would never have a career so I had to keep going however possible. I decided that for the rest of my running career, if there was any way I could get my body from A to B I would do it. This is not the advice I give to others, particularly youngsters when I chat to them, but that's the attitude I wanted to take.

It was a couple of months of absolute hell. I progressed to doing interval sessions on the cricket field, every foot plant painful, but focusing on the job at hand. I also continued with the aqua-jogging sessions, consisting of reps with very short recoveries to get my heart rate up and keep it high. One day Gav was at the edge of the pool shouting commands: Start! Stop! Over and over again. I was getting towards the end of the session, taking stock in one of the recoveries, when Gav saw me sink silently under the water. I had fallen unconscious. Gav had to lean over from the edge of the pool and drag me out. I quickly came too – I'd only been out for a few seconds – but Gav ended the session there and then. Mindful of the fine margins in gaining fitness, I couldn't stop early! I jumped back in and finished the session. That was my obsessive mentality, trying to keep my Olympic dream alive, not taking any chances.

Once I was on the road to recovery, and I believed things were truly improving, I had a scan at the hospital. 'There's quite a lot on that scan,' said team doctor Bruce Hamilton when he saw it, raising his eyebrows to indicate a huge understatement. Bruce was a doctor from New Zealand. He was good fun and brilliant at his job. Gav and I became great friends with him and his family. He subsequently used me as an example of not letting a scan determine what you can and can't do. Scans often depict a bleak image and cannot show what's achievable with a modified, flexible (and stubborn) approach.

The cross-training and cricket-field work paid off. I only started back on the track three weeks before I went to the holding camp. My leg wasn't ready, but it was now or never. Gav and I were very pleasantly surprised at the times I was achieving at the track, considering the time I'd spent away from it. I was still in pain but I gritted my teeth and went for it, and quickly started to hit some good targets in sessions. The British Olympic Association holding camp was in Paphos, Cyprus, and we were based in a luxury resort called Aphrodite Hills. I was sharing accommodation with Liz Yelling, Kathy Butler and Kelly Holmes. As the name suggests, the hotel is nestled in the string of hills above Paphos. My calf was so bad it couldn't tolerate running on any undulations so Gav hired a car so I could run round and round the flat Happy Valley Park. I was trying so hard to keep my Olympic dream alive and soon I hit a session which was pretty much on the money, doing 6 x 1,000m reps with 90 seconds in between – in racing flats not spikes. It was so hot Dave Collins, the team psychologist who later became UK Athletics performance director, stood in the middle of the track with a special hand-cooling device, which apparently had the effect of cooling our entire bodies while we recovered between efforts.

It was hard to imagine how any host city could match the euphoria of Sydney's millennium Games and its fantastic crowds. But Athens had the history of being the birthplace of the Olympics and for an athlete, an Olympics is an Olympics: it's always special. There was a lot of talk about the facilities not being ready on time, but I thought the Athletes' Village was brilliant, in spite of the hour-long bus journey to the stadium. Unusually, there were two training tracks within the village itself, so no transport to external training areas was necessary. The main track had an immaculate piece of grass in the middle, which runners ran round and round to save their legs. (Field eventers trained elsewhere.) The other track was situated in a quieter area at the end of the village. Yes, bits did look unfinished but this 'wasteland' was merely space that should have been landscaped and to me it amounted to an ideal area for some off-road running.

My heat was scheduled for 11.55 p.m., which I think was a pretty unique situation; it certainly added a bit of fun. I'd be starting the race on one day and finishing on the next! I'm not sure an Olympic track race has ever before or since started so late. Which day would I say I competed on? I'm definitely not a morning person so the timing suited me, but I noticed lots of my rivals training very late in the village, attempting to alter their body clocks.

I was pleased to qualify for the final despite the inevitable calf pain, but looking at the field for the final on paper beforehand, I realised I could run very well and still finish tenth. This was the highest standard I had ever competed at. It was going to be very challenging. Even in the heats I had had to run sub 15 minutes to qualify.

In the warm-up area just before my final, I was given the amazing news that Kelly Holmes had just won the first of her two gold medals. But there was no time to celebrate; I had to quickly refocus and line up for the final. We set off fast initially but no one wanted to take the lead and the pace was ridiculously slow. When you consider the first 200m are always fairly fast as people jostle into position, the next 200m felt like we were practically at walking pace, and we clocked a 90-second first lap. I'd never known anything like it. The next 200m was no quicker, but then two Chinese athletes, Sun Yingjie and Xing Huina, went to the front and picked up the pace. Approaching the halfway mark, Elvan Abeylegesse of Turkey put in a very fast 800m and everyone else went with her in a surge. She put in a 65-second lap, then a 66. I went too, but sensibly. Ethiopia's Meseret Defar and Kenya's Isabella Ochichi ran a 64 to catch up with Abeylegesse. This was insane pacing, more like a 1,500m race, and it didn't slow again. With only three laps to go, Abeylegesse had faded on the back stretch, leaving Defar and Ochichi to exchange the lead and ultimately battle it out for the gold. With only 200 metres to go Defar passed Ochichi and claimed her first Olympic title, finishing at 14:45.65. Ochichi took silver, and Defar's teammate Tirunesh Dibaba took bronze. I was running fast and making headway. In the final laps, I found myself running with Yelena Zadorozhnaya of Russia and we were picking off athletes. I ran about 8:36 for the last 3,000m off a very uneven first 2,000m, so I'd given my all. It was a tough and unusual race. Everyone was exhausted. And, all things considered, I was fairly pleased to finish fifth.

Not to win a medal is always disappointing when you feel you're on great form but, given my return from injury, I felt I had worked hard, given everything I had, and I had to be content with that. Tantalisingly, I had been closing in on bronze throughout the last few laps of the race. I look back and I know I gave it my absolute all on the day and finished as high as I possibly could. But I wanted more. I felt determined to try to do better ... I was both pleased and frustrated. Before the Olympics my calf was so torn I didn't go on the track for weeks and yet I achieved my best Olympic result. The Athens Olympic final was a turning point and spurred me on into 2005.

But before I'd seen out 2004, something very surprising happened: I won a bronze medal at the European Cross-Country. I'm known for being quite terrible at cross-country, and enjoy having a laugh about it. My legs seem to get stuck in the mud or slide out sideways in it! The Euro Cross is such a fun team event and my friend Hayley Yelling, who is fantastic at cross-country, won. Despite my struggles with the mud, I still enjoy the cross-country tradition we have here in the UK. As a young athlete, I used to love going to races with my Exeter Harriers teammates. Cross-country is fantastic for developing young athletes, and for strengthening you during the winter months. But I'm much better suited to a surface where there is not so much to upset my rhythm. I once had my mate Kathy Butler, who's also a great cross-country runner, fly past me on a particularly steep hill at the Edinburgh race. She looked back at me and giggled as I struggled up the hill. I love the comedy. So I did find it amusing that I had managed to pick up a bronze medal. At least it meant in future years I had some ammunition when people took the mickey out of my cross-country running. Brendon Foster once – laughingly – suggested to me and Gav that I give cross-country a miss. I have since followed that advice in my later career, but in my training, I include elements of what could be described as cross-country. Just because you're not good at something, doesn't mean you can't enjoy it.

CHAPTER 13

A Strange Sickness

After Athens I was already looking ahead to the 2008 Olympics. The Athens year had shown me that there was a possibility of winning a medal at world level, especially considering the battle I'd had with my calf injury. I was full of determination, but also aware that I was getting older. I gave an interview to a newspaper and said, confidently, that I thought I'd retire after Beijing, four years hence. That would probably be enough for me. Little did I know.

2005 was one of the years when I got into brilliant shape and was looking forward to the summer ahead. I kept my mileage high deep into the summer and travelled to Rome for the Golden League meeting with the express aim of getting a really fast time in the 5,000m. On arrival, my manager at the time, Ricky Simms, told me that unusually the Ethiopians intended to treat the race as a trial for the forthcoming World Championships, so there would be no pacemakers. I was slightly disappointed because, despite loving proper races, on this occasion I had come with one agenda: to attempt a PB. I realised I would just have to push the pace myself.

While we were in Rome, we heard the fantastic announcement

that London had won the bid for the 2012 Olympics. Wow! London had beaten the favourite, Paris, by 54 votes to 50 at the International Olympic Committee meeting in Singapore, after bids from Moscow, New York and Madrid were eliminated. Tony Blair, the Prime Minister, called it 'a momentous day' for Britain. A home Olympics is a once-in-a-lifetime event – if you're lucky – for competitors and spectators alike, so I would always have remembered where I was when we heard the news of the IOC's vote, but I recall the next twenty-four hours with absolute clarity as the mood changed from celebration to tragedy.

The next day, 7 July – the day before my 5,000m race – Gav and I had gone out for a walk to stretch our legs and get some air. We mused on the implications of a London Games when I'd be thirty-eight. Ancient! Seven years ahead is a lifetime in the mindset of an athlete focused on the current season. At the time we were thinking what a shame it was that I'd be long retired by then. But maybe we'd be coaching after starting the family we planned, and we imagined some of the stars of London 2012 would be youngsters we'd not yet heard of. When we got back to the hotel, other athletes in the foyer came up to us saying, 'Have you heard about what's happened in London?' They looked distressed as they told us of the terrible atrocities that had unfolded in the capital. We went up to the room, turned on the television and saw the awful scenes. Bombs on the tube and the bus. Like everybody else, our mood plummeted from elation to horror. Our minds were dominated by thoughts for the poor victims and their families and friends caught up in the devastation of that day. It made me stop and be very grateful for our health and happiness – and made any worries about how the race might pan out seem so insignificant.

When it came to the race the next day, difficult though it was, I had to try to concentrate my thoughts on my tactics for the race. Aware that the Ethiopians would make a cagey start, I was intent on running as hard as I could. When the gun went, none of the East African athletes wanted to take the lead or push the pace; they were there just to race it out for positions and to earn selection for their team. I ran hard, pushed and pushed. I was maintaining my pace well. Summoning up memories of my exhilarating schoolgirl races, I front-ran the race – only for about six athletes all from East Africa to fly past me at the bell. Even though I wasn't reducing my pace, it felt like I was slowing down. To run at a pace to achieve a then personal best of 14.40 and then have the East Africans take off like rockets around me was tough when I'd done all the work leading the pack, but I ignored them, put my head down and finished as fast as I could. Gav and I were thrilled with my new PB, and I was very happy to have achieved that by front-running the race. It was a great platform from which to go to the World Championships.

When I arrived in Helsinki I was running well. My sessions were going great, I was hitting my target times no problem, and I thought I had a chance to do something special. During the heats the conditions were stormy, the most ridiculous conditions I'd ever competed in at a major championships – cold, windy, with torrential rain. The rain was so heavy I could hardly keep my eyes open as I ran. The thunderstorms seemed to signal the end of the world. My friend Goldie Sayers, the javelin thrower, went to get her laundry and came back terrified by the threatening black sky. I've never minded running in hot weather, but wet and rainy conditions are not my preference. However, despite a full-scale storm raging, I ran 14:53 to qualify third fastest for the final. In the heat, it felt like we were just jogging. I couldn't recall a time when I'd ever felt so relaxed in a qualifying round, which was surprising considering the weather. I felt full of energy and was literally counting down the hours until the final.

Two days later, I woke up and tried not to acknowledge the fact I wasn't feeling very well. I had a nagging achiness down my back; my throat was a little sore. I felt weird and feverish. How could this be happening to me? I'd been training for months without a problem and, in the cruellest twist, I fell ill on the day before the biggest race of the year. I was devastated. Gav wasn't going to let me start, but I lined up despite his pleas. I don't like watching and wondering. I told myself I might be okay. The only way to find out was to give it a go. I was coming down with something so bad I can't even recall much of the race. I started and felt I could hardly put one leg in front of the other. We all know that feeling, there's no specific injury or pain, just nothing in the tank, but I'd never dropped out of a race in my career as a senior and I wasn't going to start now. I crossed the line last, my season over. I wouldn't run another step for three months.

The fluey feeling developed into a bad chest infection and virus, and then something worse. I was so weak all I could do was lie on the sofa or stay in bed all day with a severe pain at the back of my neck. The team doctors thought I might have a neurological problem. I had brain scans, electrodes placed on my head, blood tests, dozens of hospital appointments and still no one could diagnose what was wrong. I remember going out for Gav's birthday in September to a restaurant near our home in Teddington. I could barely lift the knife and fork. I was tired all day. One time we were in Newquay, we'd been to the aquarium and I struggled even to walk back up the hill into town. Gav had to help me up the hill, sit me down and go and fetch the car. I've never been ill like that before or since. It was debilitating to the extent that every aspect of day-to-day life was challenging. It was really worrying – particularly, I think, for Gav, who felt helpless.

As quickly as it came on, it then started to lift. I noticed an improvement in the first week of December and by the middle of the month, I was my old self again and soon back running. We never got a definitive answer about what had been wrong with me. It was put down to a mystery virus – one I sincerely hope never to encounter again.

CHAPTER 14

From South Africa to a Silver Medal

The 2006 Commonwealth Games were in March, which is extremely unusual for an outdoor track championship, but I thought, 'I've got to give this a go.' It was now around Christmas 2005 and time wasn't on my side. It was another one of those situations when I had nothing to lose by training hard. If I didn't make the Commonwealths, I needed to get on with it for the summer 2006 season. I'd lost so much fitness and muscle that the season might well prove to be a washout. We would just have to play it day by day. Returning to South Africa, where we had spent every winter since 2001, I faced a long road back to full fitness. I was effectively starting from scratch yet again, so it was fitting that we were beginning afresh in a new place in South Africa: Dullstroom.

The green hills of this part of Mpumalanga province reminded me a little bit of upland areas in Britain, with rocky outcrops, boulders and rolling grasslands. I loved the vast open landscapes; we'd see blue skies stretching towards the horizon on one side and storms building in the other direction. It felt very elemental with a daily, short-lived downpour caused by the warm moisture-laden air flow from the Indian Ocean meeting the high veld. The altitude of more than 8,000 feet above sea level would, we hoped, be beneficial for my training sessions.

Dullstroom lies on the road from the town of Belfast to Lydenburg in the north-east, but the roads branching off the main tarmac route are pretty much all dirt roads: miles and miles of running routes set amongst gentle hills and forest. I could run 15 miles around an area called Lakenvlei and not see another person. The isolation was broken only by the occasional passing pick-up truck, which could be annoying as they'd kick up clouds of dust. I ran mostly on my own but sometimes with Gav or occasionally with some of the Nordic athletes who trained there. They were mostly orienteers from Finland, and when they led the runs, they'd take us through tricky terrain and undergrowth as that's part of their sport. It was fun to go 'off-piste' and I thought it might do me good, though in what way I was never sure!

Our day started with coffee and toast out on the veranda of the house we rented – an old Victorian place that overlooked marshland. To one side was a lake and a very steep hill, or, I suppose, technically a mountain, given Dullstroom's elevation. After hydrating a bit more we'd head off in the car to one of our runs. There were plenty of routes to choose from, although we had two favourites: the UT trail and Lakenvlei. ('UT' was our own name for a dirt road we used for most of our training; it had a long Afrikaans name beginning with 'Ut' and we shortened it affectionately.) I enjoyed heading off in the car, listening to the Killers or U2 or something upbeat to motivate me before training. It was mostly clear blue skies but Dullstroom could have its cooler cloudy days too. After a drive of 10 or maybe 20 kilometres along the tarmac road we'd turn off onto a dirt road, drive another kilometre or more and park the car. The routes were all off-road and the landscape was varied enough that I could choose a flat run or a hilly route.

Dullstroom's claim to fame is that it is one of the coldest towns in South Africa. Although we were there during their summer months, it could get fairly chilly and we'd get the odd wet misty day at about 12°C. Mostly, though, it would be in the low to mid-20s which was great for training. We experienced some mega thunderstorms, too – very spectacular – and joked about our storm-dodging skills. We'd be sat having coffee outside at a café, note the billowing grey clouds approaching, and set off in a panic to get the run done before the afternoon storm. It made us always do our most important session in the mornings. Sometimes storms would come out of nowhere. Once, we spotted a tornado travelling towards us, devouring trees and barns. We ran as fast as we could – talk about a speed session – shouting to each other to lie flat if it reached us. On another occasion, we had driven to an area of higher altitude when a massive storm started brewing. We'd made a special journey there so we didn't want to turn back and waste the time. I ran with Gav driving right behind me on the dirt road and lightning dramatically spotlighting different pockets of the landscape. It was an incredible view, but when the lightning forks seemed to be getting nearer, I jumped in the car, feeling like I'd pushed my luck enough. We felt like storm-chasers on one of those documentaries!

To reach a track, we had to do a ninety-minute drive to the town of Ermelo. If I set off feeling nervous about meeting my targets in the track session, those worries were soon put into perspective as I looked out of the window and saw the poverty in the shanty towns: houses constructed from random bits of wood and corrugated iron sheeting, children finding immense joy in playing with an old tyre. I found the contrast between our lives very humbling, very emotional. The track facility was completely open. It had weeds growing on the inside lane, which Gav often went round pulling up before we started the session. On one occasion, a school was training at the track and I ran around with them. That brief spell of integration with the local community felt very special. As it was such a journey from Dullstroom, we'd make the most of the outing, changing out of our kit in the dire changing room to go off to Nando's for chicken and spicy rice and stocking up with a big supermarket shop.

There were no fellow Brits in Dullstroom (the British athletes who came to South Africa mostly still went to Potchefstroom or Stellenbosch, whilst others had started to go to other parts of the world like Albuquerque in New Mexico, Boulder in Colorado or Flagstaff in Arizona). But we made some great friends, such as Pekka Itavuo from Finland, who would join us on runs. On one run with him, we parked the car and saw a leopard emerge from the long grass a few feet from us and casually cross the trail. Gav and I once rounded a bend on a forest trail to find a tiny leopard cub sitting on the path. Thinking the mum might be close by, we did a quick about-turn and hastily headed off in the opposite direction. The locals thought both these animals were more likely to be servals, but I'm sticking to my leopard story. I have always sought out locations that inspire me to run, and Dullstroom, while not a place of spectacular beauty, was full of wildlife and teemed with bird life. At Lakenvlei, a sanctuary area with fairly large lakes, I'd often see eagles soaring overhead.

From time to time local kids would join in as we ran past. One lad of about ten made a particular impression on me. He wore worn-out leather school shoes but he didn't care. I was on an easy recovery run and so I steadied my pace and ran with him for a mile or so. These kids didn't have much in material terms, living in their small huts in the shanty towns, but what they did seem to have was a natural joyfulness, the type you can imagine only in Africa – I don't get small kids running alongside me in south-west London or Devon! They seemed to recognise an innocent joy in running, or perhaps it was the novelty of running with this foreigner, I'm not sure. But they always seemed so excited to see me running past; they'd be shouting, full of smiles and laughter, spontaneously sprinting alongside. They were such fun-loving kids, literally jumping out of the roadside, inspiring me.

The house we rented in Dullstroom was old and rundown but we loved it. Finnish orienteer Olli-Pekka Kärkkäinen made the arrangements for us. In the evenings it was so peaceful sitting on the large wooden veranda with a glass of wine, listening to the croaking frogs, with the reflection of the huge hill next to us playing right across the lake. A few hundred yards from the house, just over the brow of the hill, lay the shanty town of Sakhelwe. We'd often run by it, and into parts of it. I was very aware that settlements in South Africa still reflect the old Group Areas Act under apartheid. One day, I hope, we will see the redevelopment of these poor areas and a genuine integration of people, but for now Sakhelwe adjoined Dullstroom – it wasn't hidden out of view – and in chatting to the locals, what came across was the sense of community between the towns and a spirit of togetherness. During our time in South Africa, both in Dullstroom and in Potchefstroom, we lived integrated lives as athletes, coaches and physios. We had great evenings at the houses of Jean and Alta, Eben and Marijke, and Paul and Andrea who were so welcoming. But beyond our circle in sport, I was taken aback by how segregated general life was years after the official end of apartheid.

On our trips over the years I was always torn and did find it a culture shock: I've never seen such extremes of wealth and poverty side by side. It was something that continually troubled me. The poverty and crime always got to me. In our little quiet part of Mpumalanga it felt fairly safe but over time you'd hear about various crimes and road accidents and understand there is a darker side to this beautiful country. Gav and I would have long chats about it. Almost 18,000 murders a year is simply staggering and add to this 600,000 victims of violent crime and you get a chilling sense that this is not a very safe country.

Some of the troubles were close to home. In April of the previous year, 2004, the lovely Sam Haughian, one of Britain's most talented up-and-coming 5,000m runners, was fatally injured in a car crash and then robbed as he lay dying in the road. He had been to Johannesburg and was on his way back to Potchefstroom with his girlfriend Rebecca Wills. Sam was such a nice, humble guy and great company. I'd see him often in Teddington as he also trained at St Mary's University and came from Hounslow. A nice memory is Gav and I going to Maria Mutola's house just outside Johannesburg with Kelly Holmes, our good friend Anthony Whiteman (of a 3:32 1,500m PB fame), Sam and some other athletes. We had a great evening. Kelly and Maria put on an amazing barbecue, or *braai* as it's known in South Africa. Gav, Anthony and Sam larked about together all night . . . The last time I saw Sam was a week or two later in Bushy Park. He was due to return to South Africa couple of days later. He was running towards me and as we passed we exchanged a 'hi'. I had dropped Gav, who was about 20 metres behind me, and I could hear Sam laughing at him and shouting across, 'You can't even keep up with your wife!'

Sadly a car accident in South Africa also claimed my Exeter Harrier teammate Cathy Hulme, a lovely girl, who died not long after she had qualified as a doctor.

The Commonwealth Games in Melbourne began on 15 March, only three months away. We left the decision about whether to go or not as last minute as possible. As a test, I did an indoor race at the end of February in Ghent, which wasn't a spectacular time – around 8:45 – but it gave me the marker I needed. With the Games being in Australia, I had to get there at least a couple of weeks beforehand to shake off the jet lag, get to the holding camp and continue training. When Gav and I boarded the plane, three weeks before I was due to run, we were still unsure about whether or not I was going to compete. I still had a lot to do in those three weeks when, as I knew from experience, the jet lag is hard to shrug off. I would need to train hard before tapering in the last week, and that would mean going to the track when my body wanted to sleep. Fortunately, in those last three weeks my form and fitness duly started to come together. It was difficult because Gav again was instrumental in coaching and pacemaking for me, but he wasn't allowed in to the Athletes' Village. I was grateful the team staff allowed us to do whatever we felt was necessary to get me ready to compete. So Gav and I rented a flat to make things easier. It was not without a hiccup, of course. I was doing a session of 10 x 800 reps when I injured my hamstring. There's always something! So I was not as fit as I'd like to be for a major championship, but I was determined to give it a go.

The Melbourne Cricket Ground – which was built as the

centrepiece stadium for the 1956 Olympics – was the venue for the 2006 Commonwealth Games. Packed with more than 80,000 fervent fans, it felt more like an Olympic Games. There were no qualifying heats for the 5,000m. It was a straight final and I was up against the Kenyans, including the Olympic silver medallist Isabella Ochichi. Also in the field was home favourite Eloise Wellings, nine years my junior, who we saw a bit in Teddington. Buoyed by the fact that I'd even made it to the start line, I was determined to do myself justice. I had put so much into my attempts to win a medal. After so many near-misses, I had to make this one count. I was thirty-two now; I didn't know how many more championships I had left in me. But I was also not quite sure how to run the race. I didn't want to leave it all to the end, and risk having to race someone in a sprint finish as I never felt that sort of race played to my strengths. I decided to react to how I felt in the race itself – and that's what I did.

I hit the front with a few laps remaining and gradually picked up the pace. I was hoping to run away from the others, but also to save a bit for the sprint at the end. I gave it absolutely everything, but eventually had to concede to Ochichi in the sprint to the line. To my utter joy, I won the silver medal, my first outdoor major championship track medal. It had taken me a long time!

I was truly thrilled. Gav picked me up and twirled me around. It was something that together we'd worked so hard for. I love running and, despite the frustration of missing out on the medals, I'd always approached it with the mindset of appreciating all the wonderful experiences running had brought me. But I did feel so happy to finally stand on the rostrum and receive a medal. That evening I went out to celebrate with Gav and my mum and dad who'd come out to watch me. The next day felt like a dream, I had to keep reminding myself that, yes, it really did happen!

When I arrived home, I put the medal in an old shoebox. I'm not one for displaying medals or having a trophy cabinet. You wouldn't know I'm an athlete from my home – that is, if you turn a blind eye to the treadmill in the cloakroom and the piles of trainers surrounding it. I've often found myself in a panic trying to find the medals when I've been asked to take them into a school or something. However, once they're found, I believe that's what they are there for – for kids to finger and ask questions about, and perhaps to inspire those children towards their own dreams. I never worry if they come back covered with greasy handprints. It's the memories, the experiences and the work that went into winning them that I treasure.

In Melbourne we were again able to meet up with my former physio work colleagues Ross and Dana. This time we would meet their children too. It was great to be in the company of this lovely couple again and it made us realise how much we longed to start a family of our own.

However, immediately after Melbourne I would be preparing for another summer of track competition. This was still March and so I had five months to prepare for the 5,000m at the European Championships in Gothenburg, Sweden . . .

CHAPTER 15

I Wasn't Doing It All Wrong After All

That 5,000m final is a race I find very difficult to dwell on. I watched it for the first time in November 2015 with Ben Bloom from the *Sunday Telegraph*. After the news broke of a state-led, systematic doping regime in Russia, Ben asked if he could come down to Devon so we could sit and discuss the race. I agreed to do it on the understanding that it would be used as an example of how a race can turn out for a clean athlete. I didn't want an article implying 'poor me', as of course this situation had happened to other athletes too. I also knew it wasn't the only time that it had happened to me.

At the time I saw my performance in that race as a failure, a chance missed to win a medal. I was in great shape going into that champs. Just a few weeks later, I ran a lifetime PB of 14:39 at a Golden League event in Brussels.

The race itself was relatively steady. I went to the front, working hard to break up the field. I wanted to try and up the pace, to attempt to take out some of the sting of any kickers at the end. I didn't go crazy. I threw in a 2:56 km. This left just me and three others: Marta Domínguez of Spain, Liliya Shobukhova of Russia and Elvan Abeylegesse of Turkey. I was leading with that trio right behind me. I started putting in some 69-second laps to take some more out of their final kicks and then, in a flash, with 200 metres remaining, they struck and moved past me. Their freshness was phenomenal. They took all three podium places, leaving me coming down the home straight alone with all hopes of a medal snatched away. I had nothing to respond with.

I was very disappointed. I tried to rationalise it. In taking the lead, had I just taken the kick out of myself? Gav and I have always looked forwards. We had to discuss how on earth I could ever possibly compete with those performances. We had to write it off to a bad champs and didn't look back at the race again. However, nine years on, watching the race with Ben and Gav was even more painful than I expected. I had run away from the rest of the field apart from these three – and who were these three? Domínguez, Abeylegesse and Shobukhova have never been found guilty of taking drugs at the time of the 2006 European 5,000m final, but that all three have subsequently been linked with doping offences is enough to make me realise that I hadn't failed. Domínguez has been banned for three years for irregularities in her biological passport. Shobukhova was later banned for doping and, it has now emerged, allegedly bribed officials to avoid a ban. And Abeylegesse's sample from the 2007 World Championships was re-tested in 2015 and found to contain a banned substance.

When I ran a 3,000m a week or so later at a Norwich Union International in Birmingham, Shobukhova was there again. I was representing my country and there was an enthusiastic home crowd to please, but my instinct told me something was up. The Russians were being viewed with a lot of suspicion. They were achieving phenomenal times, even with unimpressive running styles. Sometimes they didn't even look that fit or athletic. I tried to ignore Shobukhova's presence in my race by running away from her, expecting the inevitable, which happened, and I came second.

No matter what else, though, I still had my silver medal from the Commonwealths. At this point in my career I had a string of top four or five finishes in major championships, with the wonderful exception of silver in Melbourne. I had a Commonwealth fifth, a European fifth, an Olympic fifth, then a European fourth, a Commonwealth silver, a World fourth. It makes me angry, looking back at those results with the knowledge that some of the athletes who consistently pipped me to the podium have since been caught doping. I lined up on every start line expecting someone to 'come out of the woodwork'. That's our euphemism for the situation.

If the 2006 track season had disorientated me a bit psychologically, that feeling took on a physical reality in the closing stages of the Great North Run. Running the last mile and a half, I felt really peculiar. I had to concentrate hard to keep running and stay upright. The road was swaying from side to side and I was almost delirious. Somehow I managed to get myself to the finish line. When I crossed the line Gav said I looked grey. I've seen photos of the volunteers holding me up just past the line and I do look ashen. Completely disorientated, I was immediately taken to the medical facilities. I kept wanting to leave but every time I got up off the bed, saying something like, 'It's okay, I feel much better now,' my legs would buckle and I'd collapse to the floor. I literally couldn't stand on my feet without wobbling and falling over. It might sound ridiculous but I felt as if I was drunk. I was very happy and merry thinking, 'What's all this fuss!' Once I'd recovered my balance some two hours after the finish, I went to see the press in the media tent. I told one reporter that I felt like I'd downed a couple of bottles of wine. This made the papers, with the *Guardian*'s Duncan Mackay writing, 'Mystery attack of "drunken delirium" robs Pavey of debut challenge'. I found this very funny to read. Even funnier was another reporter who got the wrong end of the stick. He wrote that I ran badly because I did drink a couple of bottles of wine before the race! But there was also a serious side to the incident. I went for several rounds of medical checks and my hyperglycaemia was confirmed.

2007 was a big year – and we focused on the prospects of medalling in the World Championships in Osaka, Japan, at the end of August. I knew I wasn't getting any younger, but after running that 14:39 in Brussels at the end of the 2006 season, I felt a global medal was a possibility. Gav, on top of his coaching role, also became my manager. After the galling disappointment of Gothenburg, I trained harder than ever before. We travelled out to South Africa to train during the winter months and my mileage peaked at 127 miles a week while we were in Dullstroom. During the winter of 2006/7 I would put in my heavy weeks of mileage at altitude then pop down to much lower Potchefstroom – a four-hour drive west of Dullstroom – to sharpen up with a couple of track sessions before heading home to a race.

After a week in Potchefstroom, I hopped on a plane to Stuttgart to run a 3,000m at an IAAF Permit Indoor Meeting. Normally I take a race to get going at the start of the season, but I felt great and was over the moon with my time of 8:31.50, which broke my own indoor 3,000m British record from 2004. It would have been a European record, too, if two Russian athletes hadn't run faster the year before in Moscow – one of them being Shobukhova and the other Olesya Syreva (who broke nine minutes for the first time with an 8:29, at that point her only sub 9:00).

I treasured my 8:31 straight off the back of winter running as a great stepping stone for the track season ahead. Despite a setback with a flu bug that settled in my chest, I carried my high mileage deep into the summer months. Gav just said, 'Swallow your pride. You might not do well in preparation races because we are not easing back for a summer campaign. It's all about that one race.' I had returned to the UK by May and in late June ran a 10,000m race at a British Milers Club meeting in Watford. I didn't race it as such; I followed the 31:45 qualifying pace. With about three laps to go, I felt good so I just sped up a bit and finished with a 31:26 – not my quickest, but a time I was satisfied with. I would be going to the World Championships in a new event. With that event as my focus, I competed in a few other races to benefit from the massive boost in fitness that racing gives you. I was training through these races, concentrating purely on doing well in Japan.

We flew to Macau for our final preparations before heading to Osaka. It was very hot and extremely humid and sometimes wet; in fact there was hardly ever a blue sky, but I loved that tropical feeling. Macau has a great trail along the side of a hill that was reasonably flat. Although it wasn't very extensive, the surface was ideal and I was happy repeating loops. It seemed safe from the extraordinary number of stray dogs that ran along the roads in packs and, I feared, might attack me. My first run was with Helen Clitheroe and Gav. We aimed to do a twenty-minute jog to shake off the jet lag as we had just arrived, but we ended up getting lost. Our starting point was a wooden bench, the central point for four trails heading off in different directions, and marked by stones. We'd pick a trail, head off and then end up returning to the same bench! It was like a horror film. We were totally unacclimatised. We'd gone for a simple leg stretch, with no drinks. It seemed so unprofessional, but also funny, that we kept running around and around unable to escape the bench. The image of it as we approached each time became increasingly eerie. After about ninety minutes, we tried the first trail we'd chosen but then turned off onto another trail a few hundred metres later and finally – well over an hour later – we made it back to the start point, laughing in relief at the absurdity of it all. It was very funny despite the slight worry of disturbing our carefully planned preparations. We were soaked in sweat and gasping for a drink.

The Asian heatwave of 2007 had blanketed Japan since May with temperatures ranging from 30 to 40°C. There was no let-up between day and night, and the combined temperature and humidity levels were particularly extreme on the night of the women's 10,000m final. Sitting in the stadium, Gav and Alan Storey were dripping with sweat without moving a muscle. The thermometer on Gav's GPS watch registered 36°C. With the humidity level at over 90 per cent, conditions were about as far as you can get from ideal for distance running. Just walking to the start line was reminiscent of walking into a sauna, the hot air like a physical barrier you have to push through. It was the same for everyone, so I just had to get on with it. Fortunately, I tend to naturally cope well in hot weather and, having acclimatised in the steamy hot climate of Macau, I felt well prepared.

But the race was tough. From the off, it felt like a run to the death, which would be won by whoever could endure the most discomfort. I was close to being in the best shape of my life, but it was a slow race – partly down to tactics, but mostly owing to the conditions. I felt pretty good. On the penultimate lap, I just lost hold of the leading two – Tirunesh Dibaba and Elvan Abeylegesse – but was running a strong third. The home straight beckoned . . . a medal was in my grasp. Coming around the final bend, in those last desperate throes with the line in sight, I sensed the American Kara Goucher coming past me in a late burst of speed. I pushed as hard as I could. Inside my head I was yelling, 'Come on, Jo, come ON!' but I couldn't hold on. There was nothing more to come. I gave everything. At the finish I was flat on my back, totally spent. The disappointment was huge. I felt I'd failed. Fourth was my best career placing in a World Championships, but to miss out on a medal, again, was gut-wrenching. I felt I'd let everyone down: Gav, who supported me emotionally as my husband and professionally as my coach; friends and family who boosted my spirits; supporters who had sent me messages of good luck.

As Dibaba, Abeylegesse and Goucher gave jubilant trackside interviews and waved to the crowd, I couldn't wait to get back to Gav at the warm-up track. It's times like this when I know I have the right coach. Even when I have a bad run or a disastrous result, Gav is never angry. I see other athletes suffer when their coaches go off on one, but Gav knows that I've given my absolute all. He knows how much it means to me. He will be disappointed himself, of course, but he is always there for me and knows exactly what I need to move on.

Like Gothenburg, it was another final in a major championships mentally filed in the 'tough to revisit' folder.

Eight years later, another call from a journalist prompted me to revisit that painful image of my distraught fourth-placed self. In 2015, Martha Kelner at the *Daily Mail* informed me that Abeylegesse, who had claimed the silver medal in Osaka, had been suspended for doping. Her sample from that World Championships had been frozen and retested. It had been found to contain Stanozolol, the same synthetic anabolic steroid Ben Johnson had tested positive for in the 1988 Seoul Olympics. The appeals continue still but that news – which meant the medals could be readjusted and I could receive the bronze after all – sent my emotions spinning. I had finished fourth behind someone who was cheating, who shouldn't even have been there, whose result should not and did not count. I had long had my suspicions about that race, and a few other races, because of whispers I heard on the athletics grapevine, and now I could be vindicated. On the one hand, I was thrilled to think I might get what was rightfully mine, but I was also angry. Athletes who cheat deprive clean runners of crossing the line knowing they've won a medal, of running a victory lap with a flag with the other medallists, and of standing on the podium instead of walking off the track, inwardly beating themselves up. Those are special moments, and you can never get them back.

It has a hidden impact on your career. To finish fourth or fifth, rather than on the podium, affects your confidence as an athlete. It makes you feel like everyone thinks you're always getting it wrong when it matters. You're continually having to say in interviews that, unfortunately, you weren't quite able to do it on the day, when actually it's not the way you feel inside as you don't believe in the integrity of some of the performances that you've just witnessed. It can also affect the way that you train, making you take risks, trying to attain their superhuman

levels and overdoing it. Athletes such as Goldie Sayers and the
men's 4 x 400m relay team from the Beijing Olympics, who it
now appears look likely to have been cheated out of medals,
have described how they believe that pushing themselves too
far in training to try to beat the cheats resulted in them getting
injured. Despite the introduction of the Athlete Biological
Passport in 2009 and the re-testing of frozen samples, athletes
are left feeling let down by the authorities. Stories of corruption
and cover-ups leave clean athletes feeling despondent. Funding
for anti-doping is pitiful. As an athlete I feel that not enough is
being done to truly make an impact. Frozen samples have a
ten-year limit, but you would like to think that a cheat could
never think they have got away with it even when that timeframe
has passed. Also, common sense would stipulate all anti-doping
should be independent of sporting governance and that there
should be a fully autonomous global body with far greater
powers. Every athlete worldwide should be subjected to the
same stringent anti-doping procedures. This is not yet the case.
There have certainly been many dark days for athletics, but I
am passionate about the sport, as are the majority of the people
involved in it. I don't like having to talk in a negative way about
the sport I love. The positive side of all this is that perhaps now
the huge problems have been exposed, the sport will sort itself
out and present a brighter future for the youngsters coming
through.

One day I might have a World Championship bronze medal
to add to my shoebox collection and muse on all the effort and
planning and dreams that went into it, but it will remain a bitter-
sweet moment. Did I ever question the point of pursuing glory
knowing what I was up against? Did I ever wonder why I put
myself through all this? No. I always believed that somehow I

just had to find a way to beat the cheats. I had to train harder and harder. When the gun goes on the start line, I put all negative thoughts to the back of my mind and just go for it. You never know what might happen; you have to seize the opportunity. Despite the massive frustrations, I'm not one to mope around feeling sorry for myself. I know I'm lucky to be running. It's my passion, and it's given me wonderful experiences – the travel, the team camaraderie, the satisfaction of working towards improving my performances. There is so much more to running than the results. If I wasn't trying to compete at an elite level, I'd still enjoy my runs in the forest and along the canal with my family.

CHAPTER 16

Beijing – My Last Olympics?

During the winter of 2007/8 I trained hard again with a renewed focus – the Olympic Games in Beijing. I spent the autumn training at altitude in Flagstaff, Arizona, and then travelled back out to Dullstroom for the rest of the winter. It was our second trip to the American West, having previously spent time in Boulder, Colorado, and we drove miles to our run each day before realising there was a trail right around the corner from the hotel where we were staying. Unfortunately, early in the trip, I fell over on a rocky trail and smashed my knee, which was rather stupid. We had flown out to Arizona specifically to train so there was no way I was going to rest it. It was strange to be in a desert climate where the temperatures dropped to freezing at night but rose to 25°C during the day. The change of location felt like an adventure. We've never eaten so much in our lives. When in Rome, as the saying goes . . . One restaurant specialised in a ten-course menu. If you managed to finish a course, you got another plate free. Well, that was a challenge! I ate so much I was in excruciating pain. How could I have been so daft to inflict that on myself?!

On rest days, we visited Hoover Dam, the Grand Canyon

and discovered the trails around Meteor Crater, a vast site formed 50,000 years ago as a result of a strike by an asteroid travelling at 26,000 miles per hour.

By the time we'd settled back in Dullstroom in December, I was running heavy mileages. When we left in the middle of May, I was clocking up around 115 to 125 miles per week and I was running most of this at over 8,000 feet, only dropping to about 7,000 feet for my intervals, either on a grass track in Belfast or a synthetic track in Ermelo. Training was going well and I carried this right through to the summer.

We loved our training camps in South Africa, the variety of runs in beautiful landscape, the familiarity of our routine; but the violence started to feel too close to home. I used to buy honey at a little shop called Milly's, which mostly sold trout as Dullstroom is a hub for fly fishers. The house we were renting was on the other side of a courtyard to the shop. We never heard the shots, but we were told the lovely lady who I'd often chat to during my regular honey purchases had been shot dead in the shop by her husband – while we were at home. That was a jolt. In 2007, we were back in the old rundown house with the veranda that we loved. Adjoining the house was a double garage with an annexe above. The owner let this accommodation separately, and a security guard called Wiseman lived there with two women and a gorgeous little five-year-old boy called Justice. They were refugees from Zimbabwe, very friendly, and they'd often pop in to use our microwave. We left for a quick trip to do an indoor race in Europe and on our return found they'd gone. It turned out Wiseman had shot both the women and then turned the gun on himself. Thankfully he had taken Justice to a friend's house beforehand, so the little boy was safe, but it was so devastating and shocking to realise that someone we trusted was capable of murder. The heart-breaking tragedy really got to Gav and me.

The plan for the year, as in 2007, was to focus on one main goal: the 10,000m at the Beijing Olympics. Back in Macau for the holding camp, it was nice to again be part of the team environment, going on training runs with Paula Radcliffe and Liz Yelling, and enjoying the camaraderie. Training went well for me again. The sessions were bang on, better even than before Osaka; I was ready to go. Despite the pain of those World Championships, I drew encouragement from the fact that I had finished fourth at world level. Nonetheless, I was experienced enough to know that things have to be right on the day. It's not about your last result or how training is going – even if that gives you confidence; it's all about race day. In the back of my mind, there's always a niggling worry that things could go wrong at the last minute. I would turn thirty-five the month after the Games. Would this be the end of my international career? I was pretty sure it would be my last Olympics.

In Macau, we had been as meticulously careful as ever with what we ate and obsessively used antibacterial gel to wash our hands. The nightmare would be to fall ill. Athletes, pushing ourselves hard physically and thus putting our immune systems under stress, tend to be prone to bugs, especially as we have to travel close to when we aim to peak. Gav and I arrived in Beijing three days before my race and, to my horror, I felt those undeniable stirrings in my abdomen that indicated I wasn't well. There was nothing I could do but admit to myself that I must have food poisoning or a stomach bug, and with those symptoms came weakness and lethargy. I willed myself better, but on the morning of the race I still wasn't right, better enough to think maybe I'd be okay, but aware deep down that for a professional athlete any marginal decrease in health translates into a big dip on the track. That tiny tick of the clock that seems so minuscule could be the difference between a medal and finishing down the field.

Gav advised me not to run, but, as usual, he let me make my own decision and then supported me 100 per cent. I wasn't okay at all. When the gun went, there was simply nothing there. I had no strength to muster. I got round the laps by telling myself this was an Olympic Games and I just needed to get to the finish line. I trailed in in twelfth. I felt horrendous, but thought, with a bit of time to recover, I could put it right for the 5,000m.

Part of me wanted to run out of sheer frustration, but on the day I still felt nauseous and dizzy. I tried to warm up, but was so wobbly that even in my determination to go out with a point to prove, I realised it would be insane. Gav had warned the BBC commentary team that I was going to attempt to race and explained the situation so he would know the reason if I had to make a last-minute withdrawal. When you're so far away from home, family and friends might have wondered what had gone wrong when I didn't show up at the start line. I was so disappointed. I take my team place seriously and my one consolation was that I hadn't taken someone else's place in the 5k only to pull out. There wasn't another athlete sitting at home, watching on TV, thinking they could have run the race as I had been the only athlete entered for the 5,000m for Team GB.

So that was that. My Olympics over and done with. A whole year of training to my limits, pushing myself until I was flat on my back on the track, gasping for breath after sessions, obsessively focusing on the plans and targets and tapering . . . to end the year in disaster.

CHAPTER 17

Thrilled to be Pregnant

By the end of 2008, I had not missed a single season for nine years. Despite a lot of ups and downs along the way, I'd qualified for the final in every championship I'd raced in. Considering my long battle with injuries from my teens to late twenties, that was an extremely consistent run. I was now thirty-five years of age, and gradually, my perspective on life had started to shift. I had different priorities. Always at the back of my mind I carried an image of myself as a mother, and that desire to have children became pressing. I didn't want to wait any longer. Once the prospect of becoming a mother started playing on my mind, it grew to dominate my thoughts so much that I knew running would have to take a back seat for a while. I wasn't miserable, or unhappy, but I wasn't enjoying committing my entire life to running professionally. I remember one particular day when the emotion struck me especially hard. I was training on a slightly overgrown grass track. I was working my arse off, doing three-minute all-out bursts ten times over. On that bumpy surface there wasn't any point in measuring the distance. It was a pretty standard exhausting session really, but afterwards I lay on the ground, recovering, staring up at the sky thinking,

'What am I doing? I desperately want to be a mum, and here I am still slaughtering myself.'

Having kids was so much part of our life plan that Gav and I often talked about it. As many couples do, we chatted about the names of our future children. We also discussed how we'd eventually choose to live back in Devon so the kids would have a lovely place to grow up and we could be near our families.

Our future children, our ideal family life, was something we'd occasionally drop casually into a conversation when talking about the future, but without any specific timeframe. I remember in about 2005 or 2006, Gav and I were in Berlin at an evening after-party with Ricky and Marion who were then my managers. We were talking about the World Championships, which were going to be held there in 2009. I turned to Gav and said, 'Oh, well, we won't be doing that, I'll be long retired.' I guess I assumed we'd have a family then. The same thing happened in anticipation of my mother's sixtieth birthday. Family milestone birthdays are important occasions so we'd plan in advance to make sure we'd be there and book flights around them where possible – Mum's birthday is in the winter when we'd normally be in South Africa training in a milder climate. I remember working out Mum's sixtieth would be in 2009 and thinking, 'That's okay. I'll definitely be retired and have kids by then so it won't be an issue.' Making a come back after having a child didn't seem an option. I thought I'd be too old.

By the winter of 2008, the desire to start a family became a longing to such an extent that I felt I couldn't give my all to elite running. Stopping to start a family was an easy decision for us on many levels. We were obviously willing to accept any effects it had on us financially or on potential sponsorship. Gav and I are a coach/athlete unit as well as a husband/wife partnership. We are a team. When I went on 'maternity leave', so to speak, he did too. The financial implications were simple: we had to manage with minimal income for a year. Of course this didn't matter; regardless of the consequences, we wanted to have a baby. If I got pregnant quickly, so much the better. If it took eighteen months, I would have spent the year neither pregnant nor an athlete!

As soon as Gav and I had acknowledged our desire to pause and try for a baby, and talked it through, I became ridiculously impatient. Literally the minute we decided to have a baby, I wanted to be pregnant right then. The waiting was sheer torture. I went out and bought lots of pregnancy tests weeks before I might even need them. I rationalised my purchases by buying cheap ones because I feared I might be wasting them anyway. If one did show a positive, I'd plan to go and get an expensive one to confirm it – the fancy kind that display 'pregnant' or 'not pregnant' rather than a line, and can even tell you how far along you are. I had already stopped training hard. Even before I knew I was pregnant, I only ran easy runs. I didn't feel comfortable pushing myself to the limit in case there was a newly forming foetus in there.

There I was one day, locked in the bathroom with a cheap pregnancy test, incredibly early on, and it looked . . . well . . . it was impossible to tell. Was that a line or not? A blurry mark on the white bit, or was I imagining it? I squinted and squinted, but couldn't make it out for sure. My attempt to save pennies went out of the window in a flash of excitement and I rushed out and bought one of the expensive tests there and then. Back to the bathroom and this time: PREGNANT. A plain, clear yes. I was having a baby!

Gav and I were over the moon. My priorities in life shifted immediately. All that mattered in the whole world was being pregnant. If you'd asked me about my running career, I'd have probably said, 'What running career?' If you'd offered an Olympic gold medal in exchange for being pregnant, I'd have scoffed at the ridiculous suggestion. We were going to have a baby. Neither of us was in any doubt that it was the best thing that could happen to us.

Gav and I had been together since we were teenagers, and by the time Jacob was born in September 2009 we had been married fourteen years. We took the best part of two decades to get to the point of parenthood. It was just how it worked out. When I thought about a family, I had always imagined myself as a full-time mum. I knew my priority would be our new baby and I had no idea if being the kind of mother I wanted to be would be compatible with my running career, so I knew I could be hanging up my spikes for good. The balance in my life would shift, I could be sure of that, and if it meant it became impossible to compete, so be it.

It's bizarre to think that if we'd settled down in the house near Bath that we nearly bought before we went backpacking, and had kids straightaway, they'd be teenagers by now. Parenthood has brought us so much joy and happiness. Looking back, I was terribly presumptuous. I didn't have Jacob until I was well into my mid-thirties, and Emily just a couple of weeks before I was forty, so I was incredibly lucky. Plenty of people struggle to get pregnant. I realise I was extremely fortunate to fall pregnant quickly with both the kids. With our active lifestyles, I never thought of myself as an older mum, and at my NHS antenatal class in Teddington, I wasn't one of the oldest mums. I was pretty average. Some of the other pregnant mums found it amusing that I was still able to go out for jogs as they joked how hard they found it just walking around!

Once we knew I was pregnant, Gav and I were so thrilled we didn't get bogged down with thoughts on how it might impact on my running and the logistics of it all. We were going to be parents, and we couldn't be happier. I was certain that it signalled the end of my athletic life as I'd known it, and I was totally content about that. This was a new chapter and I was excited. If I did make it back, I would stay put in the UK, race less frequently and, whenever possible, go to competitions as a family. To this day, I haven't been on a training camp since 2009 – apart from two compulsory holding camps for a week before a champs. I did wonder how a lack of altitude and warm-weather training might affect my running, but that was the way it would have to be. I wanted stability for the new addition to our family. I was looking forward to the new challenge that all mothers face: the juggling of a busy life around a family. With Gav as my supportive husband and coach, home and work were already inseparable, so I thought it might still prove possible to combine our vision of parenthood with my running. We'd have to see.

When I became pregnant, the health and safety of my unborn child was paramount. I planned to exercise through my pregnancy, not just because I'm an athlete but also because research indicates that it's beneficial for the health of both mother and baby if it's carried out safely and there are no known risk factors in the pregnancy. I was used to a high level of exercise so some easy running would not be a stress on my body. I'd be doing a fraction of my normal training regime. My agenda was simply to maintain a healthy level of fitness and conditioning of my bones, muscles and tendons. I made sure to get all the advice I could, talking to team doctors, my GP, the midwives at my antenatal checks, as many experts as I could ask, and of course listened to my body during the different stages of pregnancy as well. If someone I trusted had advised me to stop running, I would have put my running shoes away for nine months then and there. I had reduced my training load dramatically after deciding to start a family. As soon as I knew I was pregnant, I scaled back completely. Instead of running more than 100 miles a week and training twice a day, it was now a case of jogging, slowly, for a maximum of forty minutes. I completely reduced and modified my conditioning exercises. I occasionally did a bit of aqua jogging as this involves no impact. I always took many precautions. I wore a heart-rate monitor whenever I exercised and watched it like a hawk to confirm that my heart rate stayed under 140 beats per minute. I took care to be well hydrated. If I went out on a run, I would take my phone with me and let someone know exactly what route I was taking. And I would never run in the heat of a warm day; I knew it was dangerous to overheat. I also steered clear of any rough terrain to avoid the risk of a fall. The most important thing for pregnant women who are exercising is to listen to our bodies. If I felt unwell for a second, or like I was working too hard, I'd stop and I'd regularly take a few days off. I did enter one event during this period, in April 2009, when I was three months in. It was the Windsor Asthma 10k, which I ran for fun. I found reassurance in wearing my heart-rate monitor so I could see for myself how much effort I was putting in, and could run even slower if I needed to.

I often cut back because I had horrible pregnancy sickness: the kind that makes you wonder why on earth it's called morning sickness, because it arrived morning, noon and night.

Counter-intuitively, morning was definitely my best time of day so I would work around this and try to exercise then. The sickness never truly wore off but it improved. I found it interesting that although I was getting larger, aerobic exercise began to feel easier after the first three months. Despite all those thoughts about how children might be the end of my career, I still wanted to keep the door open. I didn't know if it would be possible, but the healthy fitness levels I'd maintained went some way to keeping a return to a running career a realistic prospect.

Running, easy though it was, felt surprisingly natural, much more so than I'd expected. When I imagined running while pregnant, I'd visualised a poor baby bouncing up and down inside me, but I could see that was illogical. Running still felt natural; my growing baby was part of me and when you run your internal organs don't rattle about! The human body is an amazing system designed to protect and nurture a growing life – and that includes cushioning a baby beautifully. Babies are calmed by movement. It's when you are at your most active that they tend to sleep in the womb and it's when you are lying in bed at night trying to get some sleep that they start kicking and keeping you up. Gav filmed my bump as our baby was very active and his wriggling and squirming made my belly move so much.

Morning sickness apart, I had a lovely time during that first pregnancy. Feeling healthy and energetic, I kept jogging until just over three weeks before Jacob was born. I listened to my body and, at about thirty-six weeks, I started feeling tired and a bit run down. I was checked over by my doctor and everything was fine, but the change in my energy level seemed like a sign that it was time to stop running. Gav and I just went on some nice scenic walks. Waiting for our little one to arrive, we felt more than just excited. We couldn't wait to meet this little baby. Gav and I prepared for a natural birth, hoping that everything would be okay. Gav was even thinking about what to say to me during labour. I walked around in a daydream a lot of the time, imagining what he or she would be like, who they'd take after in personality and in looks, what sort of little person they would be.

CHAPTER 18

Jacob

My life changed completely on 14 September 2009. That was the day I became a mum. It was also when the most wonderful moment in my life threatened to become the worst.

Throughout my pregnancy, I'd been happy and healthy. There were no signs that anything was wrong. I had been determined to listen to my body and wind down – and I was already taking it very easy. At around thirty-eight weeks, I went for my regular check with the midwife and she expressed some concern that the baby was a bit small for the number of weeks' gestation. She suggested a scan, simply as reassurance and to confirm all was well. She was keen to put us at ease, telling us it was purely precautionary and nothing to worry about. So even with first-time-parent nerves, I didn't worry. I'm not a big person, after all. And nor is Gav. So why would we have a huge baby? I didn't fret about it. If anything, I was a bit sceptical, and thought maybe they were making a fuss over nothing. I understood that it is always better to be overly cautious, and that the midwives are experienced, so I was grateful for her diligence. The reasoning was based on the way in which midwives inspect your bump – using a tape to measure from your belly button to pelvis, and expecting the number of centimetres to match the number of weeks pregnant you are. It seemed curiously low-tech, but clearly useful.

As an athlete, I also reasoned that my abdominal muscles are perhaps more toned, so naturally I'd expect them to hold everything in fairly tight. It's common for people who work out regularly to have small, 'tidy' bumps in pregnancy. I'd made sure that I put on weight throughout my pregnancy for the health of my baby and I wanted to make sure I could breastfeed well. But as I was still smaller than some, I reasoned that the measurements must be based on an average; and some people put on more weight than others. I figured, 'I'm smaller than average and so is my baby. Not all babies are going to be whoppers, are they?' However, we will always be grateful to the midwife who took this measurement as it proved to be the crucial starting point in saving Jacob's life.

Reassuringly throughout all of this, Jacob was kicking like mad. He always kicked and kicked. Whenever I had antenatal appointments, my tummy would be contorting all over the place as he did his mad dance and little exercises in there. The kickathon was happening the day I went in for the extra scan, at thirty-eight weeks. 'Gosh, baby's very active and healthy,' the midwives commented. I was thinking, 'That's probably why my baby's small, he or she is burning off so much energy in there!' The scan seemed fine. The doctors confirmed there was nothing to worry about, but they were still concerned about size. 'Your baby's really healthy, but we do think he's a bit small,' they said. 'So we think you should come in on Monday and get induced, so we can get him out.' As it was a Thursday and I was just over thirty-eight weeks, which is considered full term, it wasn't even technically early. The doctors explained to us that towards the end of pregnancy, the placenta – which provides all the nourishment – can start to degrade and not be as efficient as it needs to be. In this scenario, it's better to get a baby out earlier, and get them feeding and growing outside of the womb, rather than leaving them in what could be less than ideal conditions.

There was no sense of emergency. If there was, they said I'd have been admitted there and then. We were given an appointment to return a few days later, giving us a nice chilled-out weekend at home. The clinic staff were careful to emphasise the lack of urgency, so we didn't worry. The doctors anticipated that when he came out, he'd be about five pounds, which, though not tiny, is pretty small for a full-term baby, and they thought he'd thrive better out of the womb. So Gav and I went home, relaxed and reassured. Knowing our lives were about to change for ever – and that this would be the last weekend with just the two of us – we decided to have an evening out. We went for a curry as we'd heard it can bring on labour.

We'd been told to ring the hospital at 6.30 a.m. on Monday to check there was a bed as emergency admissions would take priority over getting out a baby who was just a bit titchy. The alarm went off early. We got ready, did a last-minute bag check – just in case – and rang the hospital. They told us to come in. We finished breakfast and drove to the hospital, excitedly talking about how surreal it was that we'd soon have a baby. Gav dropped me at the entrance and went off to try to find somewhere to park the car. So I walked up the stairs on my own, followed the signs and found the correct ward. The midwives showed me to a bed, stowed my bag away and told me to put my feet up and relax. Gav arrived shortly after me so we had some time alone in the room where we took final photos of the bump for our baby journal. A midwife popped in to put the trace belt on over my tummy to monitor the baby's heart rate. And she also explained about the induction process; how I'd be given a pessary containing the drugs to start my body going into labour and that it could take a while to take effect.

And then I heard someone say, 'The heart rate isn't right.'

In that split second, everything changed. A doctor, alerted by the midwife, checked the heart rate and said, 'We have to get down there now. We need to get the baby out NOW.'

I was still fully dressed in my jeans when I was handed a hospital gown and directed to the bathroom. I started to change quickly but, being very big and pregnant, I must have been a bit slow and clumsy. The urgency hit me when the midwives started banging on the door almost immediately, urging me to speed up. 'Come on! Come on!' they said. 'Hurry up!'

I barely had time to react as they hurried me along the corridor to the operating theatre. Once there, I was quickly given a spinal injection. I had to wait a short while for it to work, which felt like an eternity. I remember lying there looking at the ceiling with the medical staff again attempting to find a heartbeat. It was terrifying, awful; I felt totally disconnected from reality. I lay there powerless, with Gav at my side, desperately hoping everything would be all right, but with one thought swirling around and around in my head: 'I don't know if my baby is going to survive.' How could this be happening to us? Minutes earlier, nothing had been wrong in my world. Now everything was.

The medical staff remained calm and professional but I could read concern in their faces. I imagined they were all thinking, 'This is bad,' but I didn't say anything. I didn't want my worst fears to be spoken aloud in case they became real.

They did a C-section, and got our baby out as fast as they possibly could. After that nervous pause, we were so, so relieved when he let out his first cry. Gav cut the cord and Jacob, our little baby boy, was handed to me by the wonderful, kind Dr Larry. I gazed into Jacob's magical little face and kissed Gav. I felt huge waves of joy, more powerful than anything I'd ever experienced. We were overwhelmed with happiness. Our baby was simply gorgeous. 'He's so beautiful,' I whispered to Gav, but our relief was short-lived. This incredibly special moment was interrupted when he was quickly whisked from my arms. Jacob was making tiny distressed whimpering noises. We weren't aware of the normal colour of a newborn, but thinking back now, I remember he was extremely pale, almost white. The medical staff could see instantly he had lost nearly all his blood and they took him away at once. Where had all his blood gone?

I lay there powerless. I was still being sewn up and was literally paralysed from just above the waist down. I could hardly move a muscle. They whisked Jacob away to give him an immediate blood transfusion – but they didn't know what had happened, and whether it would solve the problem. They immediately transfused a huge amount of blood into him, and things were stable but desperate at the same time. Where had it all gone? Into his brain? His stomach? What if it had caused massive internal damage?

They tested and tested. It was the longest wait I've ever undergone. I was trying not to let my mind race. Trying not to think at all. Just waiting for the news. Eventually – an eternity later – they returned. We were so thankful he was okay. It had been very, very close, but the blood transfusion worked. He had responded. When he was born, his haemoglobin level was two: the normal level for a newborn is in a range of around 14 to 24. We had to wait a further twenty-four hours for the results of a series of tests and scans and it was a very worrying time. The doctors were still baffled, but when they took a blood test from me, and analysed the sample, they realised what had happened: most of Jacob's blood had pumped into my body. It wasn't a placental abruption, but something very rare. Some of the staff said they hadn't seen it in the thirty years they had worked at the hospital. Just a few hours before we had arrived at the hospital for our induction appointment, a small membrane between Jacob and me must have broken down, so that every time his heart beat, it pumped his blood out of him, and into me. It was incredibly rare, and usually fatal. The doctors said this could have only been going on for a short amount of time and Jacob would only have survived perhaps another two hours inside me. And there was absolutely nothing I could have done about it.

The fact that I had been booked to come into hospital for an induction had nothing to do with the life-threatening emergency that was discovered. I was purely there because he was a bit small. I'd been told to get to the hospital by 7.30 a.m., so if I hadn't needed to get up early, I may have slept in and by the time I noticed reduced movement of my baby and had actually been seen by a medical professional, it would have been too late. Somehow sheer luck saved him. It was such a miraculous coincidence that I was in the hospital for a different reason at the crucial time. If I stop to think about it – and I do regularly – the chain of events seems almost unbelievably fortuitous and it brings back a lot of emotion.

I didn't see Jacob for a while. They had whisked him off to the Special Care Baby Unit (SCBU) and I was unable to move because of the emergency anaesthetic. Until I got the feeling back into my legs, I couldn't see my new baby. They couldn't wheel an entire bed into the SCBU. I had to wait until I could get into a wheelchair. I remember desperately willing the feeling back into my legs. During this time, Gav went back and forth with our video camera so that I could see Jacob. I longed to be with him. When I could finally sort of work my legs enough to get into the chair, they took me to see him. By this time he already looked much better, but to go into a ward full of high-dependency machines beeping and see tiny babies fighting for their lives is something no antenatal class can prepare you for. I felt at once completely responsible for this tiny new life, and yet totally powerless.

We were in hospital for five days in the end – not very long, considering how ill Jacob had been. Our parents had travelled up from Devon when he was born, but were not allowed to see him for the first three days due to the swine flu epidemic. I'd always planned to breastfeed, but at first I had to express milk as they were still running constant checks on Jacob and he couldn't feed directly. The nurses had to fetch me nearly every hour during the night as there is nowhere to sleep in the SCBU. After a few days of steady improvement, the doctors agreed he was ready to go home. It was only then, when given permission to go home, that the intensity of the experience and birth – and how fortunate we had been – truly hit me. I was full of emotion as we wrote a thank-you card to all the medical staff before we left. Without them, we wouldn't have our gorgeous little boy. The 'what ifs' do haunt me. What if he hadn't been small, so we hadn't needed that induction? What if the ward had been full that morning? I cannot express how grateful I am for how things turned out and how lucky I feel. And I feel so, so deeply for others less fortunate than myself and Gav – because I know how close we came to experiencing such great sadness.

The day we took Jacob home from hospital, we felt the most enormous sense of happiness and relief. I'd been shell shocked. The panic, the surgery, hormones, his dramatic arrival, his pallor – it was almost too much to take in. One of the oddest things is that because he had so much blood transfused into him he couldn't have the heel-prick test babies have in hospital, when nurses collect a few drops of blood to test for serious conditions such as sickle-cell anaemia or cystic fibrosis. Even when Jacob was a few days old, when he was stable and healthy enough, they couldn't do this simple test on him because the blood going around his body, pumping through his veins and arteries and heart, wasn't his. It was the blood of a wonderful stranger who donated it in return for nothing more than a cup of tea and a biscuit. That simple, generous act saved our child's life.

Putting our newborn in the car for the first time was a surreal experience I'm sure all new parents can relate to. We felt we should drive at 10 miles an hour all the way home. Being a little family, finally settled back at home in familiar surroundings, was amazing.

For me, everything changed. My perspective shifted completely. Worries that had bothered me became insignificant. All that time worrying about my running targets, my training sessions, my race results! Now I was overwhelmed with happiness and love for this tiny little bundle who was dependent entirely on us. We had always had hopes and dreams for our own lives; now we had them for someone else too.

CHAPTER 19

Motherhood and Marathons

As soon as we got home we didn't have time to dwell on the worrying moments we had experienced. Every parent knows the insanity of the first few weeks with a new baby: the exhaustion of sleep deprivation, and not always knowing the difference between day and night. Interestingly, though, I think being an athlete running a high mileage helped with the tiredness. I was well used to feeling fatigued from training, and removing that was a good starting point. But I did find the early days tiring, although I think the happiness does help to get you through.

I was the first one in my antenatal group to have their baby. It was quite fun to be the first to go along to the coffee shop meet-ups actually presenting a baby. With regard to routine, Gav and I are definitely quite relaxed. We found humour in our 'go with the flow' attitude when we compared ourselves to some of our antenatal group friends who were following baby routine books to the letter. There is no right or wrong way; every parent should do what works for them and what fits with their lifestyle and values. And I don't think anyone should ever feel judged. As Jacob grew older and we established more of a loose routine, it did start to get easier, but we faced some additional challenges over the next few weeks and months.

After a few days at home, I started to find breastfeeding extremely painful. I persevered, but the pain became unbearable. When I developed a fever and excruciating pain down my back I reached for the painkillers I'd been prescribed after the Caesarean. I had stopped taking them for the post-operative soreness, but as they'd been given to me at the hospital, I knew they were safe to take when breastfeeding. The pain intensified even through the painkillers. I was overcome with weakness, so Gav packed Jacob in the car and drove me to A&E. He had to support me as I shuffled into the hospital while pushing Jacob in his pram. It was a long walk, and I collapsed inside the door. Before I knew it, I was in a wheelchair being whisked up to a ward. My temperature was high and my heart rate was over 140, which is very high for an athlete. My normal resting heart rate is around 40 beats per minute. They were worried I could go into sepsis. I was diagnosed with mastitis and stayed in hospital for three days on a course of intravenous antibiotics, with Jacob by my side, so I could continue feeding him.

It was lovely to return home again properly, although Jacob had to go back to the hospital regularly for blood tests to check his haemoglobin. It also became clear that poor little Jacob had terrible reflux. He would bring up the milk I had just lovingly (and painfully) given him, usually all over me. It not only caused piles of laundry – the least of our problems – but it caused him awful discomfort and distress, so he was more unsettled than he should have been. It was heart-rending to hear our tiny little baby in such pain. Some babies get it worse than others and Jacob suffered an extreme version of it. When I was pregnant, I'd glance through the mother and baby catalogues with pictures of babies all lovingly tucked up in their Moses baskets, beds or prams, quiet as mice and sleeping soundly by themselves. Some babies might well do that, but Jacob was definitely not one of them, the poor thing. He couldn't be put down after a feed for many weeks. He had to be held in an upright position for at least an hour and a half otherwise an entire feed of valuable breast milk would make an instant and unwelcome reappearance. By the time it was safe to put him in a more horizontal position, it would virtually be time for the next feed again.

If we risked cutting it slightly short, perhaps putting him down an hour after a feed, within seconds it would be regurgitated and he would cry. Sometimes he would vomit anyway, no matter what we did. It was so severe that when I arranged to meet other mums from our antenatal group in a favourite coffee shop in Teddington, I'd have to take four or five huge muslin cloths, and complete changes of outfit for him and me, just in case. As well as being awful for him, it was all a big palaver. I felt like I spent every moment of these groups mopping up. But it was always nice to be in the company of other new mums like Denise and Helen and for their babies, Zane and George, to become Jacob's buddies, as well as to give each other support, though they all thought I was completely mad trying to get back to running!

Our GP referred us to a consultant who gave us medication for Jacob's reflux, which he assured us would ease his symptoms and discomfort. It did, but there was an awful lot of it. For every single feed, he had to have four syringes of different medicines, all of which had to be kept in the fridge. It was a crazy time – we sometimes felt unsure about giving him so much medicine, but were assured it was the kindest thing to do to make him more comfortable. When he was a bit older we propped up his mattress with a pile of books to create an incline, which helped. We also found ourselves at the GP's at least every two weeks to get antibiotic eye drops for a chronic eye infection Jacob had come down with. But, like any parent, we just dealt with it and muddled through.

Unfortunately, there was another more serious drama to come. When Jacob was four months old, he developed a high temperature and I couldn't get him settled. Instinctively I knew something was wrong so we decided to go and have him checked out at A&E to be on the safe side. He was admitted, screaming inconsolably, so they could test him and find out what was wrong. He started to labour when breathing, and it was found that he had Respiratory Syncytial Virus (RSV), which was causing severe bronchiolitis. He also had gastroenteritis, and over the next twenty-four hours he started to deteriorate in a scary way. He was wired up to all sorts of monitors and given extra oxygen. I was expressing milk so that I could feed him small amounts by bottle as well as giving him sips of the rehydrating solution Dioralyte. By the second evening his gastro symptoms were so severe, he was taken off food. His breathing continued to deteriorate. The medical staff considered moving him to another hospital where he could be ventilated. It was all so worrying. By now, he was visibly dehydrated. The hospital was so busy there was a delay of some hours before a doctor could come and put an intravenous line in for a drip. I was so anxious, and on my own as after the first night Gav was not allowed to stay beyond the end of visiting hours at 9 p.m. Jacob was mostly asleep, but there was no way I would even consider dozing off for two minutes on the pull-out bed next to him. I scrutinised his oxygen saturation monitor literally minute by minute. The level kept getting worryingly low. His tiny stomach and the skin between his ribs were sucked in as he laboured to breathe. When he was awake, he was distressed, but his cry was silent. He was too weak to make a sound.

It was 2 a.m. when they finally came to insert an IV line. I found it extremely distressing to watch as the doctor and nurses tried without success to get a line into his tiny veins, until eventually they had luck with a vein in his foot, and went away. However, almost immediately, the line came out. The nurse called the doctor on the phone, but they had moved on to deal with another emergency. By now Jacob was seriously dehydrated. His skin was dry; his lips cracked. I knew I had to get fluids into him or he might not make it. It sounds dramatic, but I had experience as a physio working in Intensive Care wards, so I took it into my own hands to make up an electrolyte drink for him and give it to him in a sterilised bottle. He took it. The nurse was flustered as she'd only just qualified, telling me it wasn't protocol to allow me to do that, but I needed to do what I knew was right and I could see that his dehydration was becoming life-threatening. The staff were clearly overstretched at this busy time and they had been trying their best, so I got on with it myself. And slowly, slowly, Jacob started to rally. His condition was frightening for a while, and we remained in hospital for several days, eventually feeling so relieved that he was going to be all right.

When Jacob was born my mum had given me a little gift box which said on the top 'A baby is more trouble than you'd imagined, but also so much more wonderful.' This certainly rang true. The reflux continued to be tough to deal with. I ended up having to supplement him with the odd bottle of expressed milk or formula milk. I was producing more than enough milk, but he could sometimes bring back up an entire feed all over the floor. That was so frustrating. Conscious that he was so small at birth, 5lb 9oz – although not quite as tiny as they thought he would be, I worried about him getting enough food, but the consultant reassured us that he was doing well judging by the size of his thighs! Fortunately, he was happy to take a bottle. This feeding palaver went on night and day, but after ten months or so his digestion started to settle down. Even when he was getting bigger, and started being weaned on to solid foods, it was still an issue. We'd arrange to visit friends and I would think, 'Okay, if I'm taking some baby food for Jacob, I must remember not to take anything orange . . .' I was concerned about making stains on other people's carpets. As it turns out, a surprising amount of baby foods are orange.

I had started to run again fairly soon after having the C-section. The official advice is that you shouldn't do any exercise for at least six to eight weeks, but I must confess I did start earlier than that. I listened carefully to my body and felt ready to start doing something. I thought that being an athlete might make me ready to return to exercise sooner than average. I also felt that as whatever I did now was only affecting me – my body was one person again instead of two – rightly or wrongly that kind of gave me the permission to get on with it. I tried light jogging at first, feeling pitifully out of shape, but I built it up a little bit at a time. To begin with, I certainly noticed how weak my core muscles were due to the surgery. My legs felt strangely as though they weren't properly connected to my body. I ran slowly around Bushy Park, but also on the treadmill, which Gav and I had invested in to help make training more flexible around the needs of a baby. For feeding purposes I could remain at home whilst still running. I could also avoid too much running around the streets late at night in the dark on my own as the winter months set in. Our Victorian terraced house in Teddington was open plan, so the treadmill had to be in the living area, which looked quite daft, and I would always run with the curtains shut, so as not to amuse the neighbours with my crazy exploits.

We were aware there would also be impracticalities and safety issues once Jacob was crawling around so, eventually, we had a shed built in the back garden, but in the early days the treadmill came into its own as I made up my own quick-fix fitness programme. Initially I struggled to overcome the uncomfortable feeling of impact through the Caesarean scar when running outdoors, so my first workouts were to ramp up the treadmill to a gradient of 9 or 10 and kind of shuffle or race walk at a good pace. Aerobically, it was very tiring and gave me the satisfaction of getting my heart rate up to a reasonable level, something I'd avoided for so long whilst pregnant.

Trying to claw back my previous level of fitness was fairly daunting. However much I liked to think I was still fairly fit, I had inevitably lost a huge amount of stamina and muscle condition throughout pregnancy and recovering from Jacob's birth. I also had to be mindful of other postpartum issues, such as the tendency for ligaments to become looser. Gav and I talked about me returning to running, but in order to be competitive, I had the proverbial mountain to climb. To maintain a pace that a year earlier would have been something of a gentle warm-up felt impossible to begin with. It was a struggle, but also a return to something I loved. I was as exhausted as any new parent, coping with Jacob's needs round the clock, and I'd been out of serious training for the best part

Running in a home Olympics was very special. Here I am in the 5,000m, being roared on by the brilliant crowd.

The distance runners and the throwers, we joked that we looked like astronauts dressed in white and metallics!

Getting to spend some precious time with Jacob in the family lodge laid on for Team GB.

Jacob when he was just a few days old.

Taking Jacob for a little run in Bushy Park.

We were delighted to complete our family with the arrival of Emily, and we introduced her to the track early on...

I managed to sneak away from the athletes village during the 2014 Commonwealth Games in Glasgow to enjoy some family time on the beach in Ayr.

I pushed as hard as I could and was absoutely delighted to win a bronze medal in the 5,000m in Glasgow.

A very special welcome home at the airport and my bronze medal wasn't my only precious cargo. To my fellow athletes' surprise I had a baby with me too!

Arriving home to find the house decorated with England flags.

I was now 'Jo Pavey-Forty' in the media, here I'm doing an interview with the BBC, Devon-style.

Even as I crossed the line, I couldn't believe I'd managed it – my first gold medal! And just days after my bronze in Glasgow, what a fortnight...

It was so special to win a gold medal in front of my children, I couldn't wait to find Gav, the kids and my parents after the race.

Standing on the podium, hearing the national anthem being played for me was such a special experience.

Training is a bit different these days... It's a family affair,
running with Emily in the buggy and Jacob on his bike.

We try to make training fun for the kids too, Jacob has his own mini track on the beach.

Watch out Greg Rutherford – Jacob Pavey is hot on your heels!

Enjoying some family time after a run in Haldon Forest.

It's amazing to think that all those years ago I ran on this track as a junior and now I have my children playing alongside it as I train.

My priorities are different now, I love running and having the opportunity to compete, but family time in beautiful Devon will always come first.

of a year. It felt ridiculously hard sometimes, but it was a new challenge, and I kept going. As I gradually added more volume and intensity, things started to come together. All of us new mums can feel daunted about getting our bodies back to pre-pregnancy shape. I found I had to take one day at a time, be patient, and accept that my fitness regime had to be flexible around the needs of the baby, the rest of my family and my own tiredness levels. My advice is: listen to your body, don't be tough on yourself and bit by bit, you'll get there.

I was training, and keen to make my come back, but having Jacob had given me a new perspective. Running worries, like hitting targets at the track, didn't seem as important any more. Of course, I still tried hard in training, but if it didn't go as well as I'd hoped I wouldn't dwell on it. His daily routine and future occupied my thoughts. If I didn't make it back, there was something, someone, who needed me more than the world of running – a little person who made me far happier than performing well in a race.

Still, I had a goal: a target I kept reminding myself about when running felt tough. I wanted to get back and make the team for London 2012. Sure, there would be important races along the way that I would focus on, but that was my main goal. What an incredible opportunity it would be to run in a home Olympics! Day to day, though, my passion for running drove me on, loving the wonderful feeling it gave me, and being boosted by the gradual gains in fitness. From late 2009 onwards after Jacob was born, I started thinking about qualifying options for London 2012.

I loved the track but I had also dabbled in road running over the previous few years. I competed in the Great North Run over 13.1 miles – a half marathon – for the first time in 2006. As a distance runner rather than a sprinter, I am lucky to have the privilege of running with thousands of other runners in mass participation events. I find road events thrilling. After training each week in my own little bubble, it is just so uplifting to run with so many others in a great atmosphere. Road races are the most social form of racing, everyone running together, going for their own personal goals or running for important charities. My first Great North Run back in 2006 hadn't gone to plan. At the time I had never run further than 5,000m on the track. With a mile to go, I was up with the leaders when I was overcome by dizziness, and suffered my worst hyperglycaemic incident. Two years later, when I ran the Great North Run again, I hoped there wouldn't be a repeat. I ate a tuna roll about three and a half hours before, half a PowerBar ninety minutes before the start and the other half an hour before. These subtle dietary changes to add more protein to my pre-race snacks do not completely solve my unusual problem, but they go some way to alleviating it. I always make sure I travel with a tin of tuna – not forgetting the tin opener. My 2008 time of one hour, eight minutes and 53 seconds was a personal best, so I was pleased to be making progress on my road performances.

My improvement in the half marathon meant that after Jacob's arrival, I wondered about attempting a marathon. As a British distance runner, I knew that someday I wanted to experience the thrill of running the London Marathon. But London 2012 beckoned like a dangling carrot. With the distant prospect of qualifying for a fourth Olympics, and running around a stadium supported by the roar of a home crowd, it was hard not to want to get back to the track too. After all, how many athletes are lucky enough to run in the Olympic Stadium in a home Games? If the 2012 Games had not been awarded to

London, perhaps I would have hung up my track spikes and either be focusing solely on road races or retired. It's hard to know. To date, I've never seriously considered retirement. I take it one year at a time. I love running, the joy of working towards goals and the excitement of racing. Those feelings are combined with the memories of the years I lost through injury when I longed to run, but couldn't. Having the opportunity taken away from me for so long has always sharpened my appreciation of running even more. It's been part of me for so long that it's impossible to imagine life without it. And now we've found that it can fit with family life, I am encouraged to continue. Of course, I will always keep running for enjoyment – once a runner always a runner, as they say. But back then I'd already competed at three Olympic Games, surely more than my fair share! By 2012, I would be a month off thirty-nine. Gav and I discussed it and then decided to go for it.

It would be a tough slog back to full fitness, but I did at least have time on my side to qualify for 2012. Jacob was born in September 2009 so even by the time the first crazy stretch was over and I started to get back to some kind of shape, the London Olympics were still two years away. There was time to consider participating in other events, mixing things up a bit, before deciding what race I would aim for in 2012.

My first race back was in April 2010 – the Great Ireland Run, a 10k held in Dublin. Funnily enough, due to very unusual circumstances, I didn't have much time to anticipate my return to racing. I hadn't entered this race. I had planned to wait until the following month, and run the BUPA Great Manchester Run – another 10k – however the Eyjafjallajökull volcano in Iceland erupted during the week leading into the Great Ireland Run. The huge ash cloud caused the closure of most of the

European air space, which meant that many overseas athletes signed up to compete couldn't get to the event. The organisers phoned me on the Friday and asked if I could run on the Sunday so that the race had some non-Irish athletes to make up the international field. Initially I said it would be impossible as I was going to Kelly Holmes's fortieth birthday fancy-dress party that Friday night and I wasn't going to miss that. Gav was to be dressed as a knight in shining armour, and I was going as a medieval maiden. Kelly would be Queen Elizabeth I. My mum and dad had come up to stay to babysit – it was going to be our first evening out since Jacob arrived. We then worked out that it would be possible for Gav to drop me off at a hotel in London after the party so I could get up early the next morning to catch a train and then a ferry.

We had a wonderful time at the party with Kelly playing the role of queen superbly. But as if it wasn't already a crazy plan, after the party, Gav and I set off in the car so he could drop me at the hotel, only to end up at a standstill due to an incident on the M25. I checked into the hotel at 3.30 a.m. and got up again at 5.30 a.m., which made the whole thing even more crazy. I caught up on a bit of sleep on the ferry, but wasn't too confident in my preparation for the event. Despite this, I finished second – and was very happy with that result. Freya Murray ran well to win, proving strong on the tough hills. After the race, I caught the ferry back with Sonia O'Sullivan. Sonia kindly offered to drive back through the night and we chatted all the way from Holyhead to London, feeling pretty exhausted by the time we got home.

CHAPTER 20

Foiled by Stress Fractures

The signs were promising for the summer of 2010. I was chuffed that on my return from having a baby, I had won the British trials and gained selection for the GB team for the European Athletics Championships in Barcelona. But soon after, disaster struck: I developed a problem that I had not previously been prone to – a stress fracture. Pregnancy can cause the ligaments of joints to loosen. The release of the hormone relaxin is nature's way of helping the pelvic bones to prepare for birth, but the change in hormones can cause a laxity in other musculoskeletal joints. And for me, it was my feet.

During pregnancy, the arch of my left foot had 'relaxed' – kind of collapsed, really – effectively lengthening my foot. I had to wear a bigger shoe on my left foot than on the right, and the resulting changes in the mechanics of my foot had put more pressure on some of the bones. After discussion on the phone with team staff, it was decided that I should go out to the team holding camp in Portugal anyway to see if anything could be done. Gav and Jacob flew out too. But unfortunately a scan would later show that the stress fracture I had developed was so bad the team doctor said it looked more like I'd been involved in a motorcycle accident. A diagonal crack ran right through the phalanx of my big toe.

During my time in Portugal I still did everything I could to try to make competing a possibility. I went for runs and found that I could get into some sort of rhythm by heel striking and holding my big toe in the air. I went for regular physio, again to see if anything at all might help. The team were very accommodating towards Gav and Jacob. As I lay on the physio plinth, Jacob – who was ten months old by then – amused himself by pushing the laundry trolley up and down the corridor. The time came to make a decision, so I went on the team bus down to the training track in Monte Gordo in Portugal to test it out. Running slowly on trails with my toe in the air was one thing, but running in spikes around a track was quite another. I went to the session armed with various bits of foam and different inserts and a pair of scissors. I tried everything and anything, attempting to somehow come up with a way of reducing impact through my toe bone. I tried wedging bits of foam in a variety of different ways into my shoe. It was ridiculous, and unrealistic, but I was desperately hoping to find a makeshift arrangement that would at least let me run, however painfully. Once I felt I had come up with the best option, I gritted my teeth and went for it, aiming to do a lap of the track at a decent pace. The best I could manage, in considerable pain, running in a style to compensate for my problem, was one solitary lap of the track at a pace slower than I would need to do all twenty-five on race day! I was sadly ruled out of competing in the European Championships.

I felt strangely defeated. Since returning from years of injury when I was young and at the start of my career, I had embraced a new philosophy. I decided that if I was going to have a career,

I would have to find a way of running through injuries, taking each day at a time, modifying training as necessary in order to keep going in some manner as long as I could put one foot in front of the other. This was the approach I had taken with this problem – running up to an hour at a time with my toe held off the ground – but I just couldn't race twenty-five laps in spikes like that. I hasten to add I do have the bonus of my physiotherapy knowledge to help me understand what is going on and I certainly don't advise others to improvise! But I had decided that it was the way it had to be for me, otherwise I would too often be on the sidelines.

So I had done all the hard work to reach a come-back standard, put in a hell of a lot of commitment, only to have to withdraw. For me, frustration has always worked as a fuel. On a positive note, with Gav's support, I'd found that it had been possible to 'come back' from pregnancy and childbirth, and juggle training with motherhood. I won't deny it was tough sometimes. Gav and I were living 200 miles from our families in Devon – so we never had any extra hands to help out now and again. I often found myself still at the track at 9 p.m. on my own, doing sessions when the track was available and Jacob was asleep. But I felt fortunate to be a mum and that boosted my motivation.

I had worried that the balance of spending time with Jacob and training could prove difficult. If this had been the case, I know I wouldn't have felt happy to continue to run at an elite level, but it turned out the act of juggling our days and working to a new flexible routine was working out. I was able to fit in a run when he was napping, or after he had gone to sleep at night, or when Gav had taken him in the buggy to the play park, which he loved. Before Jacob was born, I woke up each morning with more of a timetable in my head. Now we were working around the needs of a baby and reacting to what each day brought. It was a new way of working, and I was enjoying it. I was extremely lucky: I felt I had the best of both worlds: being a mum at home and managing to fit in my running.

The stress fracture in my big toe phalanx took a while to settle down. I stopped doing the high-end quality work for a while, which I felt would prevent it healing, and gritted my teeth and ploughed on. Pain? What pain? I had London 2012 in my mind – although I still wasn't sure which event I should try to qualify for. Decisions needed to be made. The 5,000m and the 10,000m were still very much 'my' distances, but I was intrigued to see whether the marathon might suit me as well. To be ready to attempt my first marathon in the spring of 2011, I would have to get on with it the best I could.

At home, I was enjoying watching Jacob develop – he seemed to be moving faster by the day. He was an extremely active little boy – which is not a complaint! He was so much fun, but I noticed he was unusually energetic. I regularly met up with my antenatal-group friends in Bushy Park. The other mums sat around chatting, their little boys sitting calmly on a rug in front of them. I, on the other hand, didn't have the chance to chat as I found myself continually chasing after Jacob who would repeatedly run off into the distance. Good extra training, I suppose!

Gav and I decided I should give the London Marathon a go. I was excited. It is such an iconic event, an institution. I had watched the incredible atmosphere on television over the years and longed to experience it myself. As a British distance runner, it was something I simply had to do. I also wanted to know what it was like to run a marathon and learn about the training for a totally different event. I found the idea of a completely new challenge really motivating. Fellow runners at mass-participation races, running events, seminars and meetings often asked me for advice on marathon running. I would give what advice I could, but I never felt comfortable talking about an event I'd never done. When I went into schools, more often than not a child would ask if I had run a marathon. To answer 'no' made me feel like the child would think I wasn't a proper runner. If I was going to give it a go, I intended to fully commit to marathon training as best I could, even though I knew that coming back from a stress fracture would be less than ideal. But I wanted to see if it might be a possibility for the Olympics.

Doing those very long runs in training was a shock to the system. I had never run that far in all my years of training. I also worried about how I would pick my individual drinks bottle off the elite field table. It looked very scary on TV. It seems a bit insane in retrospect, but Gav and I set up a table with drinks bottles at the track in Teddington and I practised running past and grabbing the right one – while Jacob repeatedly threw them off the table. I hope no one was watching the daft scenario.

So in April 2011 I ran the London Marathon for the first time. You can't beat the atmosphere of these big city races – and I'd say the same about events such as the Great Manchester Run, the Great South Run, the Great North Run and many others. There is an all-in-it-together excitement which I find so inspiring. It's very uplifting to be involved in a huge collective event with people who have been training hard for their goals, running for inspirational charities, raising huge sums of money to help other people. It's humbling hearing their stories, and seeing their faces as they cross the finish line. The emotion is so raw – floods of tears, huge grins, massive hugs. The big races have such a festival atmosphere you can't help but have a smile on your face even when you have raced professionally for years.

I became so excited by the party atmosphere created by the crowds lining the streets of London, I didn't run sensibly at all. I did exactly what I would tell people not to do on their first marathon – and went off way too fast. People in the know had also warned me not to do that in the build-up to the race. However, it was billed as the 'strongest' ever women's London field and included defending champion Liliya Shobukhova (who has been stripped of her 2010 and 2011 London marathon results due to doping offences), World Champion Bai Xue of China, the 2008 Olympic Champion Constantina Dita of Romania, previous London and World Marathon Champion Irina Mikitenko of Germany, the reigning New York City Champion Edna Kiplagat of Kenya, the reigning Berlin Champion Aberu Kebede of Ethiopia, the world's best half-marathoner Mary Keitany of Kenya, and so on. Also lining up was practically the entire elite field from the Nagoya marathon in Japan, which had been cancelled due to a terrible earthquake. It was an incredible field and I wanted to be competitive and right in the thick of it. But I was being unrealistic. It was my first experience over that distance and, hampered by the stress fracture as well, I wasn't at the level to make an impact. Just as I had been warned, the pace did feel extremely easy in the early stages. I didn't quite believe just how much the pace can catch up with you if you get it wrong!

I went through the halfway point in about 71 minutes and then completely blew up to finish in 2 hours 28 minutes and 24 seconds. A nineteenth place finish. Everyone had told me to pace myself sensibly and not to go off too hard, but as an athlete you often instinctively want to push yourself and not set any limitation. I suppose I thought I'd taken it all in. I'd never experienced a race over that distance and did not anticipate the disaster that can befall you if you don't pace yourself well. It's a considerable distance, 26.2 miles. For the last 40 minutes I felt delirious. All I could do was focus on trying to finish. I did run inside the Olympic qualifying time but I was disappointed by the way I ran. I learnt my lesson. That's why you do these races, of course – to gain experience. Despite finding it tough at the end, running down to the famous finish on The Mall with the noise of the wonderful crowds is a memory that will never fade. And it's nice now to be able to talk to other runners who have made the same mistake as I did!

Later, in 2011, we targeted the New York Marathon. Thanks to the New York Road Runners, who were fantastic and welcomed us as a family, Gav, Jacob and I all went out there three times that year. In March I ran a half marathon, in June a 10k road race, and in November we all headed out again so I could compete in the New York Marathon.

Travelling the world with kids in tow has been chaotic at times but always entertaining. Before I became a mum, going to a race was calm and straightforward. I'd be picked up from my front door, driven to the airport, and then met by another car at the other end and taken to the athletes' hotel. The door-to-door service had been arranged by my sports management company and the race organiser. When Gav took on the role of my manager in 2007, he would drive me or arrange a car. I had previously considered calm and hassle-free travel a necessity in order for me to race. But the three trips to New York were great fun. The New York Road Runners, who arrange the events in the city, are a great bunch, very family oriented, and they were only too happy for us to bring Jacob along.

Taking a long flight with an active toddler presents its

challenges, as any parent knows. At the airport we did every-thing we could to burn off as much of Jacob's energy as possible. Once through security, we were set on allowing him to walk up and down, backwards and forwards, pushing his wheelie suitcase from one end of the terminal to the other, though we're not sure it had much impact! Once on board, we brought out one thing after another from our hand luggage – little toys, stickers, books – trying to make each object provide amusement for as long as possible. Unfortunately, Jacob was not interested in watching a film to pass the time, although we could occupy a few minutes with an episode of *Peppa Pig* or *Tree Fu Tom*.

On arrival, there was inevitably the challenge of dealing with the temptation of the baggage collection carousel to a young child . . . We were sure that once in the taxi heading to the hotel, Jacob would finally fall asleep, but no. Instead it was rather embarrassing as, although only eighteen months old, he cheekily repeated back everything the driver from New York Road Runners said, undermining our attempts to make a good first impression.

Travelling to events as a family makes it so much more special, as well as busier. Jacob being a very active little boy, we had to ensure he was never more than an arm's length away as he had a tendency to suddenly leg it. We spent a lot of time in Central Park so that he could run free or scuttle about on a little red fold-up bike we had taken with us. On the June trip we had fun taking him to the outdoor water play area. We went to the zoo and to the huge Toys Я Us on Broadway where Gav bought a ridiculous amount of track for the Thomas the Tank Engine set because he reckoned it was cheaper than in the UK.

Of course, I had the task of getting ready for an important race. I was grateful we had an extra room so that I could get some sleep while Gav chased a jet-lagged Jacob around the room at 3 a.m. On our final trip that year when I was competing in the marathon, the NYRRs kindly provided travel and accommodation for my mum and dad too so that Gav could focus on his coaching role with me. From our lovely hotel suite, we had the most amazing view of Times Square. Having three trips to the same city in the same year created lovely strong memories of the milestones Jacob was reaching, and it also was notable how each trip presented different challenges as he developed.

The New York Marathon was an experience I'll never forget, but unfortunately the build-up for my second marathon was again hampered. I was still struggling with the stress fractures in my foot. The New York Marathon was the first week of November and in mid-July I was diagnosed with a new stress fracture on the same foot, this time in the navicular – one of the bones at the top of the foot, near the ankle. Dr Paul Dijkstra – an extremely good doctor and friend – told me that I needed to be 'non-weight-bearing' in one of those clumpy orthopaedic boots for six weeks. I thanked him for his advice, and agreed it was correct, but explained that I had to keep going. I am always honest with the team doctors. I had a good relationship with Dr Dijkstra in that he accepted the way I work, which I appreciated, and we had a good banter about the scenario. He was definitely of the opinion that I should be in an orthopaedic boot, not putting any weight on my damaged foot at all. I'm sure he was right.

But with the marathon a few months away, stopping for six weeks followed by a tentative build-up was just not realistic, so for weeks I was in agony with every step. However, I kept going – because really, I just thought, 'What's the point in *not*?' It was 2011. I was nearly thirty-eight. However optimistic I was, I had to think that there wasn't likely to be much of my career left. I'd been pregnant, out of the sport, come back and not done very much. Frustratingly I'd missed out on the World Championships in Daegu in July that year because of the injury. So if I'd missed out on doing the New York Marathon – which was such a big target as well – then what was left? So here I was running and training for a marathon when I should have been resting and wearing a boot. I concentrated on building my volume and intensity. I also made important changes like reducing road mileage, keeping to softer trails and adding in the odd aqua-jogging session. The foot was painful for weeks and weeks, but I'd feel thrilled when I had a run and managed a correct foot plant. I'd get hugely frustrated when I couldn't get my foot 'down' on the ground properly because of pain. If I wasn't running smoothly, I wasn't running with good economy. Everything I did required more energy, and that in turn meant I'd run out of energy sooner. I might be able to run at my desired pace for a while, but I'd hit the wall sooner.

Gradually I regained more natural function in my foot and the pain started to reduce. I certainly could have done with a few more longer runs and sessions in the build-up, but I felt it was realistic to give New York a go, especially as long term I felt I needed more marathon experience. And the New York Marathon, like the London Marathon, was an event I dearly wanted to do.

When I talk to young athletes, I'm always mindful of giving the correct advice, and also talk of ways to reduce the risk of injury. But I was reacting to circumstances, too. If I had been twenty-three at that time, I wouldn't have carried on training for a marathon. It would have been stupid to risk a much greater injury early on in my career. When you are in your late thirties, every season – every big race, in fact – becomes a question of

'How much longer am I going to be able to keep doing this? Is this my last shot?'

The New York Marathon – one of six 'world marathon majors' – was a very special event in which to participate. By the time we arrived, excitement had taken hold. Okay, my preparation was less than ideal, I wasn't sure whether I'd be able to do myself justice in the race, but I was on the start line, standing, jangling with nerves, determined to do my best. It's an amazing course, New York, crossing through all five boroughs, each very different in feel. It begins on Staten Island, in Fort Wadsworth, near the approach to the Verrazano-Narrows Bridge, a double-decker road bridge. Running across this bridge is such a spectacular way to start off the marathon. The course then winds through Brooklyn for about 11 miles – running through neighbourhoods such as Bay Ridge, Sunset Park, Park Slope, Bedford-Stuyvesant, Williamsburg and Greenpoint, each with its own personality, crowds cheering and holding up inspirational signs. We then cross the Pulaski Bridge, which marks the halfway point of the race and the entrance into Long Island City, Queens. After a further couple of miles, we cross the East River via the Queensboro Bridge into Manhattan.

The race is deceptively hilly, but the bridges form a lot of the inclines so the gradients are manmade. As I approached the Pulaski Bridge, I had become separated from the group I'd been running with. It's very long, so you run above the water of the East River for a fair while. I remember it being deathly quiet – there were no spectators on the bridges – and as I went across it all I could hear was my own feet hitting the tarmac. There was not another living soul in sight. It was really quite eerie, as if I was the last person left alive in New York, like I was the character in the post-apocalyptic film *I Am Legend* where one person is left alive after a virus has wiped out mankind. Alone with my surreal thoughts, I ran off the bridge back into that wall of sound that so lifts the spirits. The climb up towards Queensboro Bridge at about mile 16 is considered one of the most challenging points and many runners begin to tire. I was pleased to gradually catch a few runners.

I put a lot of effort into my pacing strategy and made sure I ran a relatively conservative race so that this time I could finish without blowing up. I tried not to get too carried away by the incredible support willing us all on. It felt too slow at first, but that pace paid off in the later stages. The final section through Central Park – which throws a few more hills at you – was extremely tough, but the atmosphere spurred me on. I was pleased enough to finish in ninth in a time of 2 hours 28 minutes and 42 seconds. Though pretty much identical to my London time, this signalled a big improvement because New York is significantly hillier and I had felt much more in control throughout every stage of the race.

The day after the race we enjoyed some sightseeing, taking the ferry to view the Statue of Liberty, and so on – despite me hardly being able to walk. All in all, it was a great trip. I left New York feeling I had run an encouraging time, even though I would like to have run a little quicker. I understood that the stress fractures had undermined my preparations for both London and New York, so I felt like I'd love to do another marathon one day in an attempt to improve. Seasoned marathon experts say it takes a year or two to develop in the event, but I simply didn't have a year or two to spare as London 2012 was the following year.

CHAPTER 21
The Lure of London 2012

After New York, Gav and I made the decision to switch our attentions back to the track. I didn't feel confident opting to go for a championship marathon with only two (unspectacular) marathons under my belt. I felt I probably wasn't ready or experienced enough, yet I had so much experience on the track. In December 2011, we planned my preparations for the Olympics in August. The London Marathon in April would be a trial race for the Olympics but I didn't enter. The timing would only allow twelve weeks to be in peak condition for the Olympic marathon, which for me personally I knew might be problematic. One illness, or even a minor injury, and I would be up against it. I didn't want to simply take part in London; I wanted to be competitive. Gav often says that you must aim to be in the best possible shape on the day of your championship final and that all your planning should be with this in mind.

My dream was also to run in an Olympic Stadium in front of a home crowd and to do this I would have to run a track event. To do a marathon in April would make the subsequent switch to the specific type of training for the track and to adapt to wearing spikes (running in spikes is very different to running in racing flats) very difficult. But imagine if I got injured and struggled to do the necessary speed work on the track, but I was still able to put in the miles. If I'd ruled out the marathon early on, that would be my Olympic dream over. It was most sensible to keep my options open. My primary aim was to focus on 5,000m and 10,000m in training, hoping to qualify and earn the chance to run in the Olympic Stadium, but I would take marathon selection if offered it – though only after discussion with the selectors about whether I could have a little bit of time to consider which would be my best event. I would have then made a decision long before the track trials in order to give the next runner the required time to prepare. I am always adamant that my decisions should never adversely affect other athletes.

I watched the London Marathon on TV and saw Claire Hallissey and Freya Murray beat my time from the previous year and take the Olympic marathon spots. I was pleased for them – they're nice girls – and I felt enormous relief that my mind was now free to go for it on the track, no longer weighing up a complicated situation. What was frustrating was reading the newspapers the next day, reporting the strange claim that I was hoping to run the Olympic marathon and had gambled crazily on sticking with the time I'd got the previous year and not run the trial race. I mean, who would seriously do that? It would be ridiculous and embarrassing to think I had sat back in my armchair and arrogantly thought I'd definitely be selected. That would have been very disrespectful to the great girls who were competing. No one had picked up the phone and asked me why I wasn't running the London Marathon so they'd got the wrong end of the stick. Gav and I were merely using our experience to try to make sensible decisions.

While it was a little dismaying reading some of the newspaper stories, I got on with the task at hand and was finishing my warm-up at the track when UK Athletics phoned Gav to confirm I wasn't in the marathon team. I was preparing to start a session of 10 x 1,000m repetitions when Gav shouted across, 'You haven't been selected' and I shouted back, 'Okay!' I actually felt liberated by the news. It gave me huge motivation to do the session well. I was so matter-of-fact about it, Gav cracked up laughing. But it was a relief. I now knew it was track or nothing, and as my training was on target, I was reasonably confident about running well.

My first qualification race was in May, less than a month away. I was hungry to compete in London. I relish doing fast workouts on the track. It's tough at times, but it's something I've enjoyed since I joined Tony White's group back in the eighties. There is nothing like the feeling of walking off the track after a good session. The marathon would have to wait . . .

I was as surprised as anyone when my training in the first few months of 2012 went well – better than it had for years, in fact. I put much of this down to how happy I was. Coming home from a run to cuddles from Jacob put everything in perspective. I would find myself thinking about him as I ran, putting a smile on my face and an extra bounce in my stride. We had also relocated back to Devon, living in a nice little house in Tiverton while we got our Teddington house ready to put on the market. Jacob started going to pre-school two mornings a week in Chevithorne, near Tiverton. It was a big step for him and for us as he had never been away from a family member before, but he soon settled in with the help of the friendly staff. We were happy with our new set-up: Tiverton provided the perfect location for training. Our prime reason to base ourselves in that part of Devon was to access the Grand Western Canal, around

12 miles of off-road cinder trail along beautiful scenery and so perfectly maintained that there is no hindrance to running at pace. It is quiet, too. I train there to this day – meeting the same dogwalkers day after day with whom I always exchange a hello, and very occasionally another runner. I also use the superb Exeter Arena where the staff obligingly put up with our continuous phone calls to check when the track is available. I was also kindly given permission to use Exe Valley Leisure Centre. Another attraction of being back in Devon was that we could see our families more often. Our parents were now meeting up with us to play with Jacob during track sessions so that Gav was sometimes able to resume his pacemaking role which helped to lift my times.

Working up to the trials I had to make each track session count, but at this stage of my life I was taking such pleasure in watching Jacob develop before my eyes, changing all the time, always coming out with a cute new saying. People often remarked on how chatty he was. He had a great time whizzing around the estate on his scooter or balance bike going to the various play parks, and Gav enjoyed accompanying him on his skateboard. It put my running targets firmly into perspective as I prepared to attempt the qualifying time in the 5,000m and 10,000m.

As spring turned into summer, everything came together. In the course of just over a fortnight I ran the 5,000m qualifying time twice – in Manchester and then in Rome – and secured the 10,000m qualifying time in finishing second in the European Cup in Bilbao two days after the Rome race. I had to finish in the top two in either the 5,000m or 10,000m at the British Championships in Birmingham, which were doubling as the Olympic trials, and my London dream was on. I decided to run the 5,000m and after a steady, controlled race, I managed to sprint away to take the win. I'd done it. Qualified for my fourth Olympics! I was so excited. This Olympics would be extra special, not only because it was on home soil, but also because this time I knew that little Jacob would be there in the crowd. He wouldn't understand what an amazing experience that would be until he was much older, but it would be magical for me to know he'd watched me race at London 2012.

After the second stress fracture, Gav and I had decided we needed to make some dramatic changes – and now we could see they were paying dividends. Sensing we needed to take action in order to break the injury cycle and avoid the stress fracture setbacks recurring, we analysed what we thought was going on and came to some big decisions. First, we took my running back to basics. I stopped using my orthotics. I'd worked with some great podiatrists over the years who helped me get through some of my earlier injury problems, but each injury is specific. Now that pregnancy had changed my foot mechanics, the orthotics I had were no longer suitable. I also started running in more neutral running shoes rather than supportive ones. It became easier for me to be attuned to the way my foot hit the ground, and have greater awareness of when it felt correct and sense when it felt a bit 'off'. We reduced my strength and conditioning sessions from around 60 minutes to 15–20 minutes of essential work. We recognised that strength and conditioning is important but not if I was taking sore tired muscles to the track. We made sure the conditioning sessions were now very specifically tailored to help my running, comprising only functional exercises using my own body weight or occasionally very light dumbbells. Trying to achieve too much in these sessions for me personally could risk compromising my running sessions. Almost immediately, the changes paid off. I felt that I was able to run more freely. Running felt natural again. It reminded me of when I was a child, finding pure joy in the sensation of running. I could use my foot more freely and my body felt readier to run. We'd also fit my training in around whatever was going on that day with Jacob. Our training routine became more flexible. We wanted to put Jacob's needs first, so we became more adaptable – training could be earlier or later than planned to ensure we could attend a toddler group with Jacob or have a friend round to play. Over the years, I'd always had to be good at listening to my body, but now I found I had to do this all the more in order to fit round the needs of a child. I needed to have the energy to encompass so much more in life than just my running. This also resulted in me making better decisions like when to modify my training that actually helped to make it more consistent.

Gav and I continued with our usual physio routine, which fitted well into our lifestyle. When possible I always had my physio treatment at the end of the day so I could go straight to bed. I've never liked running a second session after treatment and this routine worked particularly well for me. This is one of the benefits of Gav learning to be my physio. Because I am a trained physio, he has been able to learn along the way. His ability to treat me also avoided the need to attend appointments at a clinic, which would interfere with training and encroach on time with Jacob. We had made sweeping changes with one thing in mind: to make running as uncomplicated as possible with the hope that this would eventually have a positive impact on my racing.

We were thrilled that things went well at the European Championships in Helsinki at the start of July, after missing the last two championships. The event was only a week after the British trials, and with the London Olympics just weeks away, our plans to taper my training didn't include it. But the chance to compete in another championships was an opportunity not to be missed. Throughout the race I wasn't finding the pace as comfortable as I should have, but I just kept plugging away. When the bell sounded for the lap, I was in third position, behind the Ukrainian athlete Olha Skrypak. But I managed to find something and move into second behind Ana Dulce Félix of Portugal. I came away with a silver medal. After all the problems with the stress fractures in my foot in 2010 and 2011, coming away with a championship medal could not have been sweeter. Getting older – I would be thirty-nine a month after the Games – didn't appear to be slowing me down.

The Olympic holding camp where most of the athletics team would make their final preparations was in Portugal. So the irony of the home Games was that it involved a roundabout trip for British athletes to get to the Olympic Stadium in east London. First of all, I travelled from Devon to Leicestershire to pass through Loughborough University for the 'Team GB Experience'. This involved the official kitting-out process (sixty-five items of kit, not including my race kit) and signing up to the five 'One Team GB' core values of Performance, Respect, Unity, Responsibility and Pride. I then flew from East Midlands Airport to Portugal for the holding camp on the Algarve. Each athlete would then travel directly from Portugal to the Olympic village – the travel arrangements therefore making it feel most unlike a 'home' Games!

The reason it is compulsory for all selected athletes to go to an official preparation camp is to protect athletes from distractions and have access to the physio and medical staff in case of last-minute injury niggles; and it is nice to build camaraderie with your teammates. We all went out to Portugal, which was great as it would minimise my time away from Jacob. However, it wouldn't be appropriate to bring children to the training facility so I would never consider it. Imagine if a toddler wandered off and tripped up a sprinter! But with Gav being my coach and also heavily involved in pacing me, I couldn't contemplate him not being able to be there for my final crucial sessions. In order for Gav to be able to go to the track, we'd need someone to look after Jacob during this time and Gav's parents offered to help out. They were fantastic, coming out to Portugal so that Gav could switch into coach mode when necessary. In some ways the Portugal experience seemed a bit crazy when I could have stayed at home, trained and driven up to London to compete, but we understood the benefits. We arrived late in the evening to check in at the Robinson Club Quinta da Ria, a posh golf resort, and I ran around the course late at night, determined to fit in my final preparations, however irrational it was when I could have sprained my ankle in the dark. Funnily enough, the resort was frequented by German holidaymakers. Many of the staff were German too, so the needs of the British Olympic track and field athletes were being looked after beautifully by a rival nation.

Going to the holding camp proved to be the right thing to do. My training moved up a notch. I was so relieved that I could see Jacob every day and I was able to rest and recover more than I would have with the normal chaos at home. At the training track it was very special to see the best sprinters, hurdlers and jumpers in the country doing their stuff. It was also a warm, supportive atmosphere to be in, with people who all had the same nerves that our final workouts would go well. And there was still a bit of time for banter before and after the sessions. The sprinters thought the distance runners were mad as we set off on our many long repetitions. They joked that they felt sick at the thought of our training while we were seriously blown away by their speed. It reminded me of my first Olympic experience at Sydney when I'd watched Jason Gardener and his coach practise starts for about two hours, they were laughing that he'd probably 'run' 45 seconds in the entirety of that session.

My training went well, though I still found it amusing when one of the sprint coaches said they were impressed by my style when running my sprint session. I never imagined I'd receive a compliment from the sprint team!

CHAPTER 22

A Home Olympics

Whenever I talk about London 2012, whether to friends or people I meet at events or in the playground, I realise how those Olympic Games were a magical fortnight for so many people. There were grumbles for years beforehand about how much everything would cost. The suggestions that it would be a giant waste of money and a flop were voiced right up to a day or two before the start, when suddenly the atmosphere changed. And on the night of that Opening Ceremony, directed by Danny Boyle, it totally flipped. London's Olympic Games was the most important item on the news, dominating the TV and newspaper coverage. All the traditional British cynicism evaporated overnight.

The Games were special to me, too. As a competitor, I had been to three other Olympics but I knew one on home soil would be something else. In career terms, I wondered whether this might be my last major event. Qualifying for the Games, getting to the holding camp without injury, being led out to race in the Olympic Stadium in London – these step-by-step goals had motivated me to carry on after Jacob was born. They had kept me training at a high level and pushing myself. When it was over, maybe that would be it. I didn't plan to announce my retirement the next day or anything, but Gav and I wanted another child. So I knew this could be my last year.

The only downside of being a track and field athlete is that you never get to go the Olympic Games Opening Ceremonies. As our events are scheduled to open the second week, we are still at the holding camp carrying out our final important sessions, so we always watch it together as a squad on a big screen. In Portugal, we gathered to see it in the hotel auditorium and a lot of effort went into making it a special occasion. It was nice to mark the evening with teammates like Mara Yamauchi and Lisa Dobriskey. We were all still required to dress up in the full opening-ceremony gear, which gave us a laugh. With all the metallic gold on bright white, we looked like astronauts. Charles van Commenee, the UK Athletics head coach at the time, is known for his trademark black-framed glasses and we'd all been secretly handed a mock pair to put on simultaneously to surprise him. It was a good laugh. When we left the hotel for London, the staff wished us well with banners and cheers – and off we went on the start of an incredible journey.

It was bizarre to board an international flight in order to compete in a home Games, but on arrival we were in no doubt that we'd landed in the middle of the biggest show on Earth. Security was tight. At the entrance to the Athletes' Village, soldiers boarded our coach to check it over and look at our passports. Scanning devices were run under the coach before we entered the park. These measures were reassuring, but it was also thoroughly unnerving to think that they were necessary. As we stepped off the coach, I heard a film crew earnestly giving a commentary on us 'getting off the bus'. We were back under the intense media spotlight that we'd been protected from on the holding camp.

The village itself had a busy, sociable vibe. It was more compact than others I'd stayed in owing to the high-rise accommodation blocks, which meant there was less walking involved to get to the various facilities. The dining room had seating for up to 5,000 people, which is staggering, especially when you stop to try to take in the energy of the scene: competitors of different shapes and sizes – strong wrestlers, tiny gymnasts, giant basketball players – all milling around in their national colours; food from all over the world labelled by region; loud, excited chitter-chatter. You'd have seen people on telly, providing the day's action, and there they were eating their dinner.

The volunteers, or Games Makers, really enhanced the atmosphere too. They were there for the love of helping others. They made the Games and did our country proud. It always amazed me that the enthusiastic young lads at the dining-room bag-drop area were still smiling ten hours later.

Gav stayed at our house in Teddington with his parents and Jacob. Once again, having his parents on hand enabled him to be in the warm-up area as my coach. We'd delayed putting our Teddington house on the market after our move to Devon. It was sitting there empty for a few months, but I just didn't want any distractions, disruptions or stress to jeopardise my attempts to qualify for the Olympics, and subsequently my performance in them. And we also knew that it would be useful as a base for Gav and Jacob and our extended family for the duration of the Games while I was in the Athletes' Village. As a mum, I knew the staying in the village part would be tougher now. I had been very lucky to see Jacob every day in Portugal at the holding camp, but it would be unfair on him to travel right across London every day, just to see me for a short time, during my ten-day stay in the village. I know many parents have to accept temporary separations from their children because of career commitments, but I hadn't yet experienced that and I felt unsettled by the prospect. Fortunately, the British Olympic Association provided a team lodge near the Athletes' Village where athletes could meet up with family members in a welcoming environment – with games provided for children, too – and so I met up with Gav and Jacob there on a few occasions.

My first race, the 10,000m final, was scheduled for 9.25 p.m. on the opening night of the athletics programme. It was the first track final and the crowd were up for it. I knew I was privileged to be able to run in a home Olympic Games and the atmosphere was so much more amazing than I could ever have imagined. I was intent on soaking up every sight, every decibel, every emotion. I went through the usual pre-race rituals of being sent to the call room, making sure my numbers were on correctly, tying my shoelaces, and re-tying them until I was sure they were just right.

Recalling the moment when it was time to file out of the call room and step into the full glare of the stadium still sends tingles down my spine. I wanted to press a pause button and let time stand still so I could take it all in. Minutes before we were led out, Jessica Ennis had run an amazing 200m to end the first day of her heptathlon far ahead of her rivals, so the stadium was buzzing. Standing on the start line, I again took a moment to look up at the flame, just as I had at other Games. I heard the announcer call out my name, saw my face flash up on the big screens. The roar for every single British athlete was off the scale: deafening, unbelievable, just so surreal. Did it inspire me? Of course it did! As I ran each lap, the cheers physically spurred me on, following me around each lap, pushing me to dig as deep as I could. And what made it extra special was knowing that my little boy was there.

When I qualified for the Olympics, Gav and I had decided that Jacob had to be there too. I knew that at two and a half he was unlikely to remember the experience itself, but him sitting with his dad while his mum ran in a historic Games – that was something I wanted him to treasure, even if we had to back the memory up with pictures and videos. His attendance posed a tricky issue, however, and not one most elite athletes have to worry about on the day of their final: potty training. Jacob had successfully been toilet trained a long way back, but he was still at the stage when he didn't give us much warning when he needed the loo. We'd get two minutes, if we were lucky, or else disaster struck. Gav realised that once they were inside the stadium, installed in the seats the family had been allocated, he wouldn't be able to dash with Jacob and make the loo on time. There needed to be a plan to try to avoid issues arising during my actual race. As a precautionary measure, we decided it would be best to put a nappy back on Jacob for the evening. Jacob himself didn't mind in the slightest as he sat with Gav next to the parents of my teammate and fellow 10,000m runner Julia Bleasdale. He wasn't fazed by the big, loud, party atmosphere and he certainly didn't have much of a sense of occasion. Guess what he did during most of the 10,000m final? Yes, he filled that precautionary nappy. It was pretty obvious what he was doing – holding the seat in front, straining – leaving Gav and the other families around them cracking up with laughter. There's nothing like a toddler for creating comedy during a nervy occasion.

Of course, I didn't know about any of this until after the race. I'd lined up – as I had for well over a decade now – intent on running as well as I could. I was thrilled to finish in 30 minutes and 53 seconds – a big personal best. Amusingly, my time stands as the official world record for a woman over the age of thirty-five – a milestone I'd passed several years before.

I finished seventh, behind three Ethiopians, two Kenyans and one former Ethiopian running for Bahrain. The East Africans have long been dominant in distance running, so I was particularly pleased to be the top-placed non-African runner.

Just behind me, in eighth, was Julia Bleasdale, who ran absolutely brilliantly to set a PB too. It was lovely to have a teammate to celebrate with. Egged on by the crowd, we did a final lap together for a bit of fun for the home fans. After the race I found Gav and Jacob, and really wanted to go home to Teddington with them, but I had to stay in the Athletes' Village until I had finished racing. That was tough – an extra thing to deal with – but it was also an honour to be a member of Team GB in the village. And I had the 5,000m heats to prepare for.

I quickly received physio at the warm-down track, then went back to the village to eat and have an ice bath to help with my recovery. My calves were extremely sore immediately after the race, but they were even more painful the next day. I am well used to getting sore calves – that's why I wear my knee-high compression socks when I race, regardless of what they look like. I get a lot of problems, not because my calves are weak, more due to my tendency to overuse them (because my hamstrings don't do enough work), and sure enough, I could scarcely walk. I didn't even attempt any recovery running the day after the race as it was impossible. I wasn't upset; it was almost comical. I had always known that ending up in this state was a likely outcome. The Olympic track is much harder than a traditional Tartan track because it's designed for sprinters like Usain Bolt and it feels like rock when you're pounding on it over twenty-five laps in spikes. In addition, in training I'd never do 10,000m work in spikes; I'd do some of it in racing flats. So I rested, had physio with Neil Black and regular ice baths, doing all I could, but I had only three days until my 5,000m heat, and that wasn't enough time for me to run pain-free. On one day I went to the team lodge to spend a bit of time with Jacob – and also to get down on the floor and have an extra emergency calf massage from Gav! But the 5,000m was another opportunity to run in a home Games in that incredible atmosphere, just a few days after Super Saturday when Jessica Ennis, Mo Farah and Greg Rutherford won gold for our country, and there was no way I was going to withdraw through fear of injuring myself.

The problem with the heats is that they are very tactical, as qualification for the final is the goal and a field of thirty-six narrows to fifteen. That means plenty of bursts of speed and unexpected moves to cover, but my calf problems made it virtually impossible to manoeuvre quickly. I qualified but not as comfortably as I'd have liked. It then took me an unbelievably long time to walk from the stadium back to the warm-up track. I didn't even attempt to do a warm-down. I just couldn't run another stride. The warm-down was more of a social session. I was perfectly cheerful, remembering my mantra as a mum – I can only do what I can do.

I didn't know realistically how competitive I could be in the final. I was so desperate to run as pain-free as possible in order to do myself justice, I experimented wearing two layers of my long socks. My spikes didn't feel comfortable with two pairs on, so I cut off the foot sections and wore two layers on my calves.

In the warm-up, I didn't do my strides. I couldn't. I just jogged. But, again, the atmosphere was electric. Once more, the crowd gave me extra motivation, a crazy wall of sound almost pushing me around the track. I don't think I've ever been more aware of a crowd willing me on. It was phenomenal and it was so rewarding to find I could run smoothly and take the pace. Again, I finished seventh in 15 minutes, 12.72 seconds, and the winner was Meseret Defar. Again, Julia was one place behind me in eighth. And again, the athletes who finished in the top six all hailed from Kenya and Ethiopia.

After the final, there was no way I was going back to the village. I'd packed an overnight bag so I could head back to Teddington, straight from the warm-down track, but in my excitement I completely forgot to collect it. Jacob had been to see my 10,000m final, but we'd decided once was enough for the experience. He'd seen me run in the Olympics and, being so young, we didn't want him to endure all the crowds and travel again. We'd ticked that box, so he'd stayed with Gav's dad who had kindly volunteered to babysit so Gav's mum could experience the Olympics (he had been to see the heats). I was so desperate to see Jacob I jumped straight on the train from Stratford, still in my Olympic kit. While we were on the train Gav phoned to arrange a takeaway curry before our favourite Indian in Teddington, the Bilas Tandoori, closed for the night. There I was on the Docklands Light Railway, ordering a chicken Balti with onion bhajis, naan bread and lots of poppadums on a train full of people, a great number of whom had just watched my race. And I was hardly inconspicuous in my Olympic kit! When we arrived back at the house, we discovered that Gav had forgotten to give his dad a key, so he and Jacob and been stuck in the house all day. We checked on them – snoring away together on the double bed – and then Gav, his mum Sheila and I tucked into our curry. It was surreal – sitting in my own dining room, eating my favourite curry, still in my kit, having just run an Olympic final.

Then I realised I'd forgotten my overnight bag! I had to text a team official to ask if it had been picked up from the warm-down track and taken back to the village.

The next day was both lovely, in that I spent wonderful quality time in my old family house, but also embarrassing. Because the house was about to go on the market, it was empty apart from a few essential items, so I had no clothes there. I had arranged to meet up with Denise, a friend from my antenatal class, with Jacob and her son Zane and I turned up wearing clothes from an Olympics goodie bag I'd given Gav to bring home from the team lodge a couple of days previously. Thank goodness I'd done that or else I'd have had to wear the competition kit I'd travelled home in the night before! I'd usually wear normal clothes to meet a friend for lunch, but I turned up in brand-new sports kit with a colourful Union flag on the front, which screamed, 'Look at me, I'm an athlete.' But I had no choice!

Later, I went back to the Athletes' Village for the Closing Ceremony. We had a fun team photo before we left the village, and it was a great evening. Athletes had a prime position for the spectacular show, standing in the in-field, and we were all finally able to relax.

Two seventh places weren't my best Olympic performances, but I was very satisfied to be the first non-African athlete in both the 10,000m and the 5,000m. Ironically, I felt more competitive in the 5k, and afterwards I wondered if I might have achieved a higher finish position if I hadn't run the 10,000m days before. But then I'd run a PB in that. It was encouraging that I definitely wasn't slowing down at thirty-eight.

The year ended on a high. I was very pleased to win the Great South Run, one of my favourite road races, for the second time in my career. There were a lot of positives to take away from London 2012 – most of which would come to fruition two years down the line.

CHAPTER 23

Emily

We'd always planned to have more than one child. And now Jacob was getting to the age where a sibling felt like a pressing issue. While my running was going well, time was ticking by and Gav and I both felt it was the right moment to expand our family. Not knowing whether my running career was over for good or not, we decided to move to our final family home in a lovely village near Ottery St Mary in Devon regardless. I would be further from the canal running trail but we had to think of our family life too, and I knew it was likely as I approached forty that I was probably as good as retired from competitive running. Jacob would soon be getting to the age where his name would need to be put down for the local primary school, and we wanted him to be settled with friends at the village pre-school. We soon settled in and have made some great friends here.

Again, we were very lucky and I got pregnant pretty much straightaway. This pregnancy, though, was much tougher. I'd had rather horrible morning sickness with Jacob, but it was worse second time around. People said this can be the case if you are expecting a girl as there are more female hormones circulating. I don't know how much truth there is to that, but it definitely seemed true for me. It was also a bit daunting knowing at the outset that I had months of nausea and fatigue ahead of me, even though I knew of course it would be worth it. The first time you get pregnant, you have no other little one to care for. Now we had another child to look after and I wanted to spend quality time with Jacob, knowing that life would soon be a bit crazy for him as well as us once we had a newborn in the family, so I chose to do less exercise during my second pregnancy. I also knew that this time round, with Jacob to consider, there would be less time to rest. I continued to jog most days for a maximum of 40 minutes, taking days off when I felt tired, as I had done in my first pregnancy, but I certainly didn't have the time to add in the odd aqua-jogging or stationary bike session.

The pregnancy was difficult at times. I had terrible insomnia and sickness so I'd sometimes be up half the night lying on the sofa, gazing blankly at the TV. The nausea often felt like it was going on for an eternity, but when I look back now, it seems like a sliver of time.

Emily's birth on 4 September 2013 was a far more straightforward affair than Jacob's. I had elected to have a C-section because of what happened with Jacob. I would have loved the chance to experience a natural birth but I didn't want to take any risks. My only concern was to bear a healthy child. Gav and I again had that surreal feeling going to bed the night before, knowing we'd have a new baby in the morning. When we were expecting Jacob, we hadn't found out in advance whether he'd be a boy or girl. This time we knew we were having a girl. Thanks to Jacob, we had also known her name for a long time too. He was the first person we told when we learnt at my twenty-week scan that we were having a girl. Emily had been one of our favourite names, but Jacob immediately began to refer to my bump as 'Emily' and often asked in the morning during my pregnancy whether 'Emily' was 'out yet'.

While we went to hospital with pink sleep suits rather than neutral ones this time, the emotions were the same when our new baby was handed to me. Gav and I were overjoyed. We looked into her little eyes. She was perfect, not as small as Jacob had been, but still quite a titchy 6lb 4oz.

As a baby, Emily was much luckier than her brother and didn't suffer from the distressing reflux that had caused him so much anguish. We were now a family of four, with all the happy chaos that goes along with having a young child and a baby. Jacob loved having a sister and has always been great with her. In between seeing to his needs, feeding Emily, trying to keep up with domestic chores and snatching some sleep, it was time to get back on the treadmill again. Could I possibly maintain a running career now I was a mother of two?

Gav and I discussed the situation and decided to give it a go. We thought it would be lovely if I could represent the country just one more time. It was probably unrealistic, I thought, given that I wouldn't allow running to encroach on enjoying time with my newborn and breastfeeding her – especially as the trials for the 10,000m were in May 2014, earlier than for other track events.

When I'm at a big road race, I love being able to chat afterwards to runners from all walks of life. People often ask me how I juggle my training around being a busy mum, and with 'being old'! I admit things are crazy at times, but in a positive way. At this later stage of my career it's nice to share stories with other runners who are also managing to fit their athletic lives around a family. I can truly relate to that now. Earlier in my career, all I had to do was focus on running. I used to go on training camps all over the world and my routine was simply a matter of training, eating, sleeping and going out for a civilised coffee. Now, apart from the compulsory holding camp in Portugal, I haven't been away on a training camp for more than seven years; it's just Gav and me working away together as athlete and coach in Devon. When I'm training I still push myself hard, trying to hit targets just as I always have. In many ways I push harder, feeling like if I'm to take a bit of time out of parent mode, I want to make it worth it. But the rest of the time I'm a busy mum at home. It has been a nice surprise to me that the huge switch in lifestyle hasn't compromised my performance in the way I thought it might, and that I am enjoying life more. I know I am very lucky to have Gav's support. He's my husband, my coach, physio and best friend all in one. We have always been a team in everything, from getting the kids ready for the day to preparing my running schedule and I couldn't do it without him. With Gav's help I can fit my training around the kids and get it done somehow, whether that's me popping out for a run, going on the treadmill, or us all going on a family outing to the track, canal or forest in the daytime – however hectic it might be. I know I'm fortunate that our sort of work-from-home situation, although rather chaotic at times, means we have been able to juggle things between us, and we feel extremely lucky to have lots of quality time with the children. Since becoming a mum I have found things have changed in the way I work both physically and mentally that have enabled me to combine being a mother with fitting in a serious amount of miles each week.

These days I treat a run or an interval session as a regular part of my day. It's something I do and I'll fit it in somewhere.

Psychologically, being a mum has been helpful for me. It made a refreshing change to no longer have the time to worry in advance about how the sessions were going to go. I don't dwell on it; I simply put on my kit and get on with it. I'm not one for strict timetables; I'd be permanently stressed if I felt a compulsion to run at precise times. Running is part of my daily routine but it's flexible, fitting in around the needs of the kids, incorporating parties and play dates and trips out. I find I manage to squeeze in training one way or another, whether it's early morning or 9 p.m. (that's when the treadmill comes in handy). The mundane tasks in life often have to take a back seat. Sometimes you have to walk past the laundry pile and ignore the dirty dishes until later. On the whole, though, I take multi-tasking to an extreme. It may sound insane but I often do some strength and conditioning work, or core stability work, and do domestic chores in the short rests between exercises. It's a good use of time. I can do an exercise then check on the dinner, then do some more, or deal with a few items of laundry. People would laugh if they saw it in action – and I'm not suggesting it's particularly professional! Flexibility with training has always been an important part of our approach, but as I've grown older it's taken on added meaning, and it's now the bedrock of my continued participation at a competitive level. We runners can become fixated on our routines – having to run at a certain time, in a certain place, in certain conditions. Now? I go with the flow. When I'm out with the kids, I often have kit packed in the car in case I want to fit in a run somewhere random, rather than come home early to fit it in. I can't always guarantee a nice flat road route or trail to run on. My backpacking days taught me to see potential training terrain in a variety of different places – whether that's a sandy beach (good resistance) or hilly trails or a cricket ground – and I extended that view to time as well as place. Before I had kids I used to get more rest between training sessions. Now I often find myself chasing the kids along the beach or around parks or indoor play centres. Surprisingly, I think keeping constantly on the go has done me good. It definitely helps with the stamina!

We regularly make training a family affair, all of us going to the track, the forest or the canal. I love that we can do this for many reasons. We can enjoy keeping fit as a family and show the kids that it's fun to be active – and yet I also get my training done. It's so much nicer than being off on a run on my own. I find it enjoyable, motivating and life enriching. We particularly love going to Haldon Forest and the Grand Western Canal, both a twenty-five-minute drive away. Although, as every parent knows, getting out of the house with young kids is something of a military operation. We have to get them ready to go out, pack everything they need – drinks, snacks, spare clothes, bike hats, nappies, wipes, toys and so on – as well as pack everything I need for training. Anyone who knows Gav and me would agree that we are superb at mislaying stuff, so it's pretty chaotic as we rush around, running up and downstairs like yo-yos, trying to find everything. There is definitely huge room for improvement in our ability to get out the door! Gav then has to put the bikes on the rack and running buggy in the roof box. Eventually we get going, music on in the car, playing the soundtrack to *Frozen*, *The Lego Movie* or Moshi Monsters songs. On arrival we go through the procedure of getting the running buggy out of the roof box, and Jacob's bike off the bike rack, and Gav's bike too, if Emily is going on the bike seat on the back. Finally, after putting on coats and bike hats, we're off.

Jacob is pretty good on his bike. In fact, if we're not careful, he can end up too far in the distance. So he has now been well drilled to know the stopping points he must keep to on our favoured loop of the forest and at the canal he knows to keep us in sight. This became imperative after a worrying experience when we were on holiday in Cornwall. I had gone on my own with Jacob to the Camel Trail for a run. He would normally keep me in sight, but he got overexcited about being somewhere new and took off on a downhill tarmacked stretch. I was shouting his name frantically as he disappeared into the distance. To my relief, a kind man who was out on bikes with his own family gave chase and retrieved him. I certainly made sure I reinforced the rules for future outings!

Going on runs as a family has evolved from Jacob at first being the one in a running buggy or on the back of a bike, to then hanging back with Gav as he was mastering the skill of riding his own bike, to now being able to leave us all for dead! Emily meanwhile loves being in the buggy or on the back of the bike, watching the world rush by. After the run we can spend time in the sandpit at the kids' play area and have a picnic. Emily rushes to see the huge wooden carving of the Gruffalo. At first she wouldn't go anywhere near it: now she loves it. Jacob, meanwhile, can spend a lot of time having fun on the BMX course.

Another challenge as a track and field athlete is to arrange the day around when the track is available. I can't always use it when I want to, especially in the summer when there are so many school bookings and sports days. So Gav or I ring up at the start of the week, find out when we can use it and then formulate my training schedule. Gav will ring to find out about other tracks in Yeovil or Plymouth if necessary during crucial times of the year – although these are both a good hour's drive away.

The way we operate our track sessions with the kids varies. In the early days, it was impossible to be away from the baby. Now the situation is more flexible. We are there as a family of four pretty regularly, but sometimes I do a morning session and we may just have Emily now that Jacob is at school. Occasionally our parents join us at the track, or either set of parents will come over to our house to babysit so that Gav can do a bit of pacemaking for me at the track when it comes to the crunch before a championship. When my kids are at the track, I enjoy the session more. Jacob sometimes wants to join me on the warm-up and warm-down. Emily now does the warm-up with Gav in a running buggy, then has a go at running herself, with her cute little skipping style. Gav will often put out some little plastic hurdles and do some fun things with the kids on the side straight while I finish my warm-up. Sometimes Jacob does quite a lot of exercise at the track, sometimes he hardly does any at all and just plays on the grass bank. It's up to him. He has fun going to clubs like tag rugby and swimming with his school friends. We want to let our kids try different things as they get older, and support them in the things they enjoy. If they want to run, we'll obviously give them our backing but the main thing is to encourage them in their chosen passion.

Day to day, for me to have my husband as my coach is a huge advantage. He is so supportive and, in addition to that, he makes it possible for me to be the mum I want to be by adapting our routine around family life. We've worked with some great coaches, but I wouldn't be comfortable picking up the phone to another coach to say, 'Actually I'm going to be at the track two hours later than we planned.' It wouldn't be fair to them. With Gav as my coach, if everything has to change and my schedule has to be adapted, it's pretty easy for me to stroll into the next room and discuss it with my coach! My training routine becomes more rigid as important races approach, but at certain times of the year, I like to work hard but have even more flexibility with actual days as well as time of day. The kids' needs and their happy childhoods are my top priority.

Most parents agree that when you look back on the days before children you wonder what on earth you did with all the free time you used to have. How did you fill the day? I find the busier I am, the more efficient I become, albeit in our own rather hectic way. I've stopped worrying about the small stuff because I am focusing on what has to be done. I try to eat healthily – that's important in helping your muscles to recover after a hard session. I have my recovery drink at the track. But if I call in at the supermarket to get a meal deal on the way home, it's not the end of the world.

I've discovered that in relaxing and allowing myself a bit of leeway, I've achieved more than I thought was possible. I train hard but my priorities have changed, which I can see has been beneficial for my running. Before big training sessions or a race, I would use up time and energy to add more stress to what I was about to do. Now, I simply don't have that option. Before an important training session, or in the last few days before a race, I'm more likely to be organising play dates and school runs, making sure there's enough clean laundry and school clothes for rest of the week. I have found that having to make decisions about juggling training around the needs of the kids and having fun with them has actually made me make better decisions regarding my running.

I'm more likely to listen to my body, as I need energy for life in general and not just for running. I enjoy the banter of being an older runner and it's very complimentary, but to me age is just a number – as clichéd as that sounds. I still just try to get the times at the track like I always have. Gav and I have been working together as coach and athlete for many years now, and we realise that the great thing about getting older is that we're able to use the knowledge and experience we've gained and find what works best for me. We frequently wish we had known when we were younger what we know now as it would have been so helpful!

Our approach isn't merely about the sessions. It's about how the whole training mix fits together to suit me. The training itself involves a mixture of long runs, tempo runs, interval sessions, recovery runs and some strength and conditioning work. And I ensure I take a rest day. The interval sessions are based around a system using a range of different paces. My ability to run a certain speed at shorter distances impacts on my ability over longer distances. Gav writes a progression chart with times we aim to achieve in training for certain distances, depending on the type of session and the recovery times. We gradually work towards these training targets as the trials and championships draw nearer. Throughout the year we don't follow the traditional 'periodisation approach' which, in brief, is when you concentrate on volume in the winter, transition in the spring and then increase the speed work in the summer. My work is still high volume in the winter, but with faster work too, so there is a more subtle change of emphasis. We find this not only helps with preventing injury, but also avoids the panic of playing catch-up if you've lost too much pace throughout the winter months. However, something simpler lies at the heart of our training methods. It's our flexible approach, our ability to respond and adapt to situations as they arise. It's all based on what I can actually do on a given day and not blindly doing what I think I should be doing. It's about keeping everything in real time and not sticking to stuff written on a piece of paper. This has helped me go from missing many years in my early career to becoming consistent. Consistency is the key to reaching your potential, or at least to getting close to it. I believe our flexible approach enables me to achieve repeatable units of training, helping to make it more sustainable. The training can then become progressive over time as I gradually become more conditioned and adapt to what I am doing.

I used to be the sort of athlete who wants to push on and Gav is there to control the whole process. Gav motivates me, but he doesn't have to push me. It is more likely that he will have to hold me back. He is good at long-term planning whilst at the same time adapting and responding to outcomes. We aim in our training for being able to sustain a pace for a distance but also to be able to race. This requires a delicate balance between endurance and speed work.

I have spent many years going to championships and it's flattering to be asked for advice on how to start running later in life and make fitness a priority. People often say they find it a daunting prospect to take those first steps but, as long as you don't have a medical concern, your age, shape and ability are irrelevant and should never deter anyone. Running is such an inclusive sport and you only have to watch a big road race to see this. I have heard such inspirational stories about people who've used the Couch to 5k running app that you can get free from the NHS website. For example, people who at first could only manage a couple of minutes of jogging and walking but a few

months down the line have entered their first race. In addition
to the health and fitness gains, running boosts your sense of
well-being, confidence and self-esteem. Aim to make running
part of your daily routine, but listen to your body and be flexible
with your schedule. If you're completely new to running, don't
feel you need to keep running continuously to begin with. Start
by trying to run for a few minutes, then walking for a few
minutes and then running again for a few more minutes and
build up gradually. Don't run every day to begin with, and even
when you're more accomplished, always take your rest days.
Set yourself a goal, like running your first ever 10k – this will
sharpen your motivation, giving you a reason to get out of the
door. Have mini goals along the way, too, to keep you going.
Your local Parkrun would be a fantastic event to try: Parkruns
are open to everyone and taking part is a great experience. You
could also join a running group to enjoy the social side of
running. Having that camaraderie will give you a boost as you
motivate each other. When possible take the time to run in
beautiful surroundings and vary your running routes. I find
running enriches my life in so many ways. The enjoyment and
experiences it has given me have always made me want to
continue, whatever level I'm running at as I get even older!

I consider it one of the great privileges of my career to be
involved in a sport that has a strong mass-participation culture.
There are plenty of sports that are amazing to watch, inspirational, fun, exciting, even moving, but many other sports have
an 'elite' level that you watch and an amateur level that you can
take part in – but not at the same time. You can cycle a stage of
the Tour de France in advance, but you can't line up with the
peloton for a stage. The great thing about distance running is
that so-called 'elite' runners line up in fields of thousands for a

marathon or road race, and I'm so pleased to have seen that part of the sport flourish. The atmosphere is totally different from when I first started. I love taking my own family to these events when I am racing because they feel, now, like proper days out. Everyone who is running seems to have a family member shouting for them, and it's magical to see the homemade banners being held up by little children who look so proud when their mums goes past. What great role models. Perhaps it will inspire the children to join a club like I did. Maybe those children will grow up to be competitive athletes. Maybe they'll run for fun and a sense of well-being. These parents running, putting themselves out there, are teaching children great life lessons too: that it's good to try something, to practise, to improve and to achieve a goal, and that being active and healthy is fun.

Emily was born in September 2013, the same month I turned forty, such a happy, special time. During those early weeks of managing a newborn's sleep pattern – or lack of a pattern, I should say, as there wasn't anything regular about her sleep/ wake cycle – I felt like I was permanently jet-lagged. But you know as time goes by it will get easier. For the first few days after a C-section, things are also tough as it's hard to bend in the middle. And, you can't use your hands to push yourself up from a chair when you're holding a baby, so things can be a bit tricky. Jacob turned four ten days after Emily was born. He was enjoying going to the local pre-school two days a week and was so proud to tell everyone about his baby sister. We arranged a birthday party for the whole of his pre-school class and plenty of others at our house. Friends thought I was crazy, but it was fun. I wanted to make sure Jacob enjoyed his birthday, especially with so much attention being showered on his new sister. I do remember feeling particularly sore as we shopped for the food and goody bags. Luckily Gav's mum is well known for her amazing cakes, so that was sorted in advance.

Training was low on my list of priorities in the initial stages. I was breastfeeding Emily on demand through the day and night and enjoying quality time with Jacob. Given that I had gone through nine months of pregnancy and given birth again by C-section, I needed time to rest and recover. If only!

Gav and I had decided that I would try to make a come back. London 2012 had shown us that I could still run well on the track and now, in 2014, at the age of forty, I wouldn't be that much older . . . I didn't want to retire from athletics without giving it one more go and, in 2014, there was the lure of both the Commonwealth Games in Glasgow and the European Championships in Zurich to tempt me. Women who have had children will recognise the longing to 'get your body back' after giving birth and I, too, had a sense of urgency about regaining my pre-pregnancy fitness. Surely this would be my last major championships? How much longer could I realistically keep going? I had nothing to lose by giving it a go, did I?

Old habits die hard, and I was soon running – again, at first, trying to shuffle along on an inclined treadmill. Our treadmill was now housed in a tiny box room just inside the back door, surrounded by hanging coats and shoes. I have to clear the way around the moving belt before I start to ensure no loose shoes get caught in it. Friends have often remarked that I must be very motivated to train in what is, in effect, a cupboard! But it allows me to clock up my mileage indoors at home, which was crucial at that time because it meant I could hop off at any minute to feed Emily again. Gav and I obviously prefer to be outside, but the treadmill is definitely a useful adjunct to training.

My first run outside after Emily's birth was in the forest. We chose a straight stretch so that I could go up and down rather than going out of sight. Gav pushed Emily to and fro in the pram, whilst Jacob played around on his bike. I ran back and forth, knowing I could stop and go to the car if Emily needed a feed. One strategy I tried in the very early build-up was to directly relate my training to my levels of sleep. If I had a reasonable night's kip, I would aim to run a bit harder or longer the next day. If it was one of those nights where Emily wouldn't settle, or Jacob was poorly or had a nightmare – or a combination of both – then I wouldn't do more than a very light jog. With two small children, I was always going to have the odd terrible night and, even with a healthy quotient of sleep, I could never rest as much as I might like to. But I felt mentally relaxed, knowing I could only do what I could do, and what would be would be. Up until Christmas I didn't even keep a training diary, I just reacted sensibly to the circumstances each day. Gav and I had learnt a lot from my first come back when I had worked back to a good level only to end up with a stress fracture. We had slightly underestimated the effect that pregnancy could have on ligaments and bones and we vowed to do everything to ensure this didn't happen again. So many times in my career we have been able to learn from our experiences.

They say that having two kids is more than twice the work of one – and I agree! It creates even more juggling and multi-tasking. But at least we were fortunate that with Emily everything had been straightforward, and this time there had been no health issues with either of us.

I knew I'd have to come in the top two at the 10,000m National

Championships to qualify for the European Championships, and I was also hoping to do enough in the early part of the season to be selected for the English team for the Commonwealth Games. I needed to get into much better shape. And fast. While I had doubts about my physical condition, one thing had not changed. I was as keen as ever to wear an England and GB vest, and to represent my country again.

Medals were a long way from my mind. They weren't on our radar at all. I was still breastfeeding. And unlike Jacob, who had taken a bottle fairly early on when he needed extra feeds, Emily absolutely refused. She was a chilled-out, happy little baby in every way but the one thing she absolutely would not do was take a bottle. That was just not, ever, going to happen as far as she was concerned. That combination of stubbornness about one thing and a relaxed attitude to everything else was a trait I confess I recognise fully! While I was breastfeeding, I couldn't ever stray too far from her.

Before Emily was born, I had accepted the honour of acting as starter for the Great South Run in Portsmouth in late October. It's an event I love and, not being able to run it myself, I jumped at the opportunity to be involved. I anticipated Emily being nine weeks old by then and assumed Gav could give her a bottle of expressed milk, tucked away in the comfort of a hotel room with Jacob, while I did my official duties on the rostrum. As the date approached, however, I started to panic because Emily was just not going to have anything to do with a bottle, and I knew I'd be up on the rostrum for more than an hour, marking the start for the staggered time slots of 30,000 runners. To make matters worse, a nasty storm was predicted to strike the south coast and Gav didn't want to be wielding a baby, a very active four-year-old and a pram along a seafront in squally conditions. But there was no other solution: Gav would have to bring both kids to the start on Clarence Esplanade in Southsea and position himself so I could be close to Emily.

On the day, everything went better than expected: Emily fell asleep. 'All is calm,' I thought. 'I can enjoy the great honour of starting the race for all these runners.' But, literally thirty seconds before the start, Jacob scrambled up a rock and was blown off by a gust of wind. He cut his head and had to go to the first-aid tents. It just showed us, no matter how much you plan with children, you have to expect the unexpected! Throughout the event, the wind intensified and we had a scary struggle afterwards walking back along Old Portsmouth seafront with the pram about to take off!

As a spectating official, I found the Great South Run so inspiring. I couldn't wait to get back out there at an event. As I made my way back to fitness, Emily's feeding remained something that had to be worked around. I could run from the door and take my phone, ensuring I didn't go too far, just repeating a very small loop. But because the other training venues involved a drive, we continued to go as a family, with Gav, Jacob and Emily following in my wake on wheels of some sort. It was fun, fitting in my training in wonderful scenery with my family enjoying it too. Otherwise I had my trusty treadmill.

At first I simply ran. I gave no thought to pace or target times; I was trying to recapture the feeling that this is what my body does, this is what it's designed to do. Running in beautiful surroundings as I often do in Devon was a boost. I would be running under trees with the sunlight filtering through, past fields with grazing cows or sheep, next to hedgerows full of birdsong. Appreciation of the scenery lifted my mind from thinking about how unfit I felt and allowed me to work towards recapturing that perfect state of 'flow' that all runners aim for, be they Olympians or fun runners. It's a state where running feels effortless and your body and mind are instinctively in tune. But if I was going to qualify for, and compete at, a major championships then I needed to get 'track fit' again, too.

In early 2014 we were unexpectedly presented with a huge challenge. We heard news that our local athletics track in Exeter would be closed from March to September for resurfacing! The whole season! I feared this was one barrier too many. The nearest alternative running track was in Yeovil, a good hour's drive away. It was going to make it tougher than we'd first imagined, but I had to accept it. It was simply another obstacle to overcome.

The people who run the track in Yeovil were wonderful. They trusted me with my own key so that we could come and go as we pleased. That helped enormously, as all my training sessions had to be timed around the children, particularly Emily's feeds. So the whole family came along. The journey there often wasn't the greatest, winding along the A30 and the notorious A303 through the Blackdown Hills. The A303 is the main route to London and the south-east, despite much of it being single lane. Often in the summer it can be very busy, so our one-hour drive to Yeovil sometimes turned into a ninety-minute crawl, as we sat in slow-moving traffic or were stuck behind a tractor. On any car journey with kids you have their antics to deal with. I sat in the back to entertain them, often feeling quite travel sick on the winding roads. We would time the drive so that Emily would need a nap, so she would hardly notice.

On arrival in Yeovil, we'd get the kids out of their car seats and wander down to the track. At this stage Jacob was not yet old enough to jog the warm-up laps with me, but part of my warm-up routine before I do my main running is to do drills. He could join in with these. They can look pretty funny, even to adults, with their big over-exaggerated steps and stretches. Jacob would find warm-up exercises like a walking lunge or high-knee steps hilarious, and try to copy them – which regularly had us in tears of laughter. Once the main session started, Jacob would be sprinting up and down the runway of the long jump while Gav was coaching me, a sleeping Emily strapped to his front in the baby carrier with a stopwatch in his hand calling out my splits. As she got older and the weather grew warmer, Emily would sometimes sit playing with toys on a rug by the finish line.

Although they were relaxed family affairs, feeling far removed from your typical elite athlete set-up, those track sessions were also some of the hardest sessions I've ever done. There were days when I was trying to hit certain times, for 1,000m reps, say, where it just felt impossible, like I was moving through treacle. I was so much slower than I had been in 2012, I didn't know whether to laugh or cry. At the start I was something like 20 seconds slower over 800m. It might not sound too bad, but believe me, it was galling, a huge margin to try to make up. How could I ever think I'd be able to qualify for the European Championships and Commonwealth Games? Gav would remind me that however slow I still felt, I *was* gradually getting my fitness back, I really was, and that things would start to feel easier soon. I was also encouraged along by Jacob shouting, 'Go on, Jo!' which used to make me feel like laughing as I was running round. Normally he would always call me Mummy, but he was copying his dad. One weight off my mind was that the children enjoyed our family training outings. After the session, if the weather was nice we'd sit on the grassy area next to the track and eat our picnic. There was a lovely play park there too which we'd use before getting back in the car. Instead of going for a rest after training I'd now find myself crawling through the pirate ship. Emily was so little she was content anywhere, while Jacob loved running around making up games and sprinting up and down. I stopped worrying and began to enjoy our novel training set-up. I could train and have fun with my children at the same time. It was fairly tiring, however, as by the time we arrived home, it was almost time for my second run of the day. But slowly things started to come together.

In late spring, my fitness suddenly 'clicked'. Sessions no longer felt quite so tough. I was still working hard but my body responded well. My running felt natural, fluid. It is no coincidence that the first week of April was when Emily was weaned. I felt happy that I'd managed to breastfeed Emily. It had been my main priority, whilst trying at the same time to regain my fitness. I also felt fortunate to be able to breastfeed, as I know for some mothers this doesn't work out. Emily was seven months old and was progressing with solid foods. That left me a month or so to get 'race fit'. My body needed to be back in tip-top shape for the European trials on Parliament Hill on Hampstead Heath on 10 May. The revelation for me was that, despite the comically short timeframe – an urgent deadline if ever there was one – I didn't stress about it. Before I became a mother, I would have been uptight and anxious about reaching my training targets, measuring my progress, worrying a session could have gone better; but I didn't have the time to dwell on it. I was so busy keeping up with Jacob and Emily's schedules, I didn't have the headspace even to count the sessions I could get in before the big race. If I made it, if I got the time, won that race – fine. If I didn't? Well, I had other things to occupy my life now, other concerns.

Until I had children, any stress I felt almost always came from running. What else did I have to fret about? Each session at the track, each planned tempo run, would be the focus of my day. I'd think about it from the moment I got up in the morning even if the session wasn't until the evening. The intensity of the pressure I put myself under meant that even one second off pace, or a fraction under my planned target time, would be such a disappointment, ridiculous though that now seems to me. After the arrival of Jacob and Emily, I had a far better appreciation of what truly matters, a far healthier perspective. Running is something I work hard at but my family is the centre of my universe.

CHAPTER 24

Full Circle

That windy evening on Parliament Hill was the beginning of a summer that will define my career for the rest of my life. My first track race since the Olympic final in August 2012, my first race of any kind since the Great South Run in October 2012, my first race since my lengthy lay-off for pregnancy and birth, and it was not a low-key one to ease me back in gently, it was the European trial and National Championships. What on earth was I thinking? When I crossed the line, I was elated to become National Champion and to qualify for the European Championships on the wrong side of forty. It was also comical to be wearing my old Exeter Harriers vest from my teenage years – thanks to Gav's laundry skills. Winning that race had felt mad. At the time I would have been pleased with that result as a high point of my year.

Exactly a week later I ran in the British Milers Club 5,000m in Watford. It seemed crazy to be doing a race again so soon after a 10,000m but I wanted to get a qualifying time for the 5,000m for the European Championships and the Commonwealth Games. It was actually my only chance to get a qualifying time for the Commonwealths before the deadline. I declined the kind offer of a pacemaker and stuck rigidly to my lap times. I came home having achieved the qualifying time and, quite amusingly, a new over-forty world record of 15.11. My next race was the Rome Diamond League; it proved a tough race and I was a bit disappointed with my time of 15.04 as I was hoping to run better in a top-class event. Nevertheless, it was solid and I'd broken my own over-forty world record. I must confess I would have had no idea of the fact that I'd got these records unless I'd been told in Watford. It added a sense of fun to the situation and helped to start off my geriatric status!

A few weeks later was the European 5,000m trial in which I came second behind Emelia Gorecka, a very promising young-ster who, at twenty, was half my age.

So now I had two cracks at a major event separated by only ten days. The logistics involved for Team Pavey – athlete, coach and kids – suddenly struck us as somewhat hectic. We would all travel up to Glasgow from Devon, and then make the journey to Switzerland with all the kids' kit and caboodle. What was I expecting to come away with? Athletes want to win medals, but I was forty and taking it as it comes. I would give it my best. I was not thinking about my medal prospects. I could only expect the unexpected.

With three weeks until the Commonwealth Games, I had one more race to get out of the way first. And it was an important one. As I lined up at the start of my final race before the championships, I felt incredibly relaxed. No nerves at all. It was a beautiful sunny day and all the spectators were friends and little children from the village wearing pumps, shorts and sun hats. I looked around and saw Jacob sitting with his friend. Gav was standing with Emily, who had fallen asleep in the pushchair, and chatting to another dad. It was the mums' race in the pre-school sports day.

Funnily enough, I'm not that competitive a person, though as a professional athlete it's something that most people expect of me. I couldn't care less about who wins a board game, or a game of snap. But I did win the race and we all had a good laugh about it showing I was in good shape for the Common-wealth Games.

Jacob won his race too. As parents of a four-year-old, we were more surprised that he did what he was supposed to do and ran from A to B. He had a burst of that amazing energy that only little children seem to have. I wish you could bottle it. He started slowly and then just hurled himself forward, arms flailing, legs kicking furiously. He didn't even look around him. It was a fun day, with the kids trying everything, and it was lovely to see them enjoying themselves.

Having my family around me and living a normal life as a mum makes me relaxed and happy. In planning logistics for the Commonwealth Games, we tried to find the right balance between family time and training, always making sure the kids would have an enjoyable time. I would have to stay in the Athletes' Village but if they were staying close by, I could nip out to see them.

Researching accommodation options close to Glasgow, we found a holiday village up on the Ayrshire coast, south-west of the city and the Commonwealth Games venues. In contrast to a cramped hotel room, with fewer facilities, toys and home comforts, a proper family holiday village with a beach, swimming pools and playgrounds seemed the perfect solution. Gav's mum and dad joined Gav in their static caravan, which was a great help. It's really important to me that the kids hold these times as precious childhood memories. I want them to remember the fun they had. I don't care if they are only half interested in my race as long as they enjoyed the waterslides and the ice cream at the beach nearby. The reality of event traffic and road closures meant my planned daily meet-up wasn't going to be as easy as we had anticipated. It wasn't going to be a good idea for Gav to drive over each day with Jacob and Emily, but they did manage it a few times and on other days I travelled by train to where they were staying. It was a beautiful area and it did me a lot of good to relax, unwind and feel happy; but I must admit it felt rather odd being on the beach one day, building sandcastles with Jacob and walking down to the sea, with such a big race pending. All in all, though, I was pleased it fitted well with training. I only had a short afternoon run to do, which I did on the most amazing grassy area behind the beach – saving my legs from the tarmac by the Athletes' Village. Nevertheless, I decided to keep my beach trip quiet back at the village . . . I was used to having Gav at my training session to pace me, encourage me and shout out my times, but with Emily being so young and the travel to the facilities being so tricky, I'd adapted to being more self-contained and was so much more chilled out knowing that the rest of my family were having fun. I even sneaked back the odd bundle of dirty baby clothes to stick in the mesh laundry bag I'd been given to hand in at the athletes' laundry facilities, to save Gav that chore.

On race day itself, Helen Clitheroe, Emelia Gorecka and I walked to the transport area together to get on the coach to the stadium for the 5,000m Commonwealth Games final. It's great to have teammates to chat with at these nerve-racking times. My life as an athlete and a mum had reduced the worry of achieving training targets, but it's pretty hard to lessen those fairly daunting feelings when it comes to the crunch of actually going to a championship race. Years of racing had at least helped me learn how to channel my nerves in the right direction. I also knew my new priorities in life would make me happy with the result whatever it was. Still, I was pretty nervous when we arrived at the warm-up track. The weather was awful, with monsoon-like rain. We headed to a Portakabin to take shelter until it was time to warm-up. Many athletes who were to be competing that night had the same idea so it was ridiculously crowded. Some people were chatting; others had headphones on and were in their own little worlds, listening to calming music or pumping themselves up, zoning out the chatter. Helen and I sat together on a bit of floor that we were lucky to find. We'd been friends and teammates for so long, having been at many of the same races and championships over the years, and several training camps in Potchefstroom. It was extremely special to be sharing the experience with someone I'd known for so much of my career. We joked about being the oldies of the field and agreed it doesn't get easier as you get older. We instinctively knew how each other was feeling too, that indescribable moment when you're at the championship venue and the clock is ticking down to the race. After all those months of preparation, we'd soon be on that start line. 'What are we doing?' we were saying. 'Why aren't we retired? Why are we still putting ourselves through this torment?' We were, of course, thrilled to be there. It is why we both toil at training year after year to make it to the championships of the sport that we love, but having a light-hearted moan sometimes helps as a coping strategy.

Going out to warm up, the rain remained torrential. It wasn't the ideal scenario for our final preparations for a championship race. I tried to avoid running through puddles of deep water, but to no avail. My long socks were soaked and I felt foolish that I hadn't taken them off for the warm-up. I did have a spare pair, but I figured I'd just get wet again anyway, and I wasn't keen to change them as I'd stuck nice England flag tape on the front of the ones I was wearing. It was almost a relief when it was time to gather in the call room forty minutes before the race and wait to be shepherded out to the track. We were all gathering ourselves, getting focused on the race ahead, when an official came up to us and solemnly said, 'Just to inform you, the race is still going to go ahead.' That cracked us up. Like we ever, for a second, thought that a bit of Scottish rain would stop the race! It's totally understandable when technical events like the pole vault have to be cancelled but very rarely a 5,000m, but it was also the timing of his announcement that was amusing – to tell us we weren't going to race at that late stage would have been slightly crazy.

By the time we walked out, the rain had stopped and the organisers had done a great job of sweeping the water off the track. I was pleasantly surprised by what a good state the track was in, considering how bad the weather had been.

I have run in a lot of major championships, but as I'd learnt at the London Olympics, nothing can beat the roar you get at a home games – even as an English athlete competing in Scotland. At this Games, it was affectionately known as the Hampden Roar. The crowd was fantastic, very supportive. Gav and his dad had Jacob with them in the stands. As a precaution, they had brought an iPad ready to play *Ice Age* as a last resort. We had decided to leave Emily, now ten months old, at the holiday park with Gav's mum because the noise might have been too much for her. Besides, I was presuming this to be my swansong year, and so we planned to take her to the Europeans ten days later. As the TV cameras came around, zooming in on one athlete at a time, and the stadium announcer called my name, the roar of sound brought back memories of the reception that greeted us at the London 2012 Olympic Stadium. I waited, and waited, feeling that sense of calm I finally feel when all there is left to do is race. The pistol went bang.

We were off. Most of the crowd assumed that this was surely going to be another Kenyan 1–2–3. Their dominance in endurance events gives them an aura of invincibility. But what did I have to lose? When I'd discussed the race with Gav beforehand, I had said that I was just going to run as though I was trying to get a medal, regardless of whether it ended up with me blowing up and finishing the race at the back. If I ran cautiously – just making sure to finish in a reasonable position, not risking anything – then no one is going to think, 'She might be one to watch for the future.' This was it. This, quite probably, was my last season of competing in major championships. I could travel back to the memory of the girl who first fell in love with running and race like young Jo Davis, racing freely, going for it with no fear, and seeing what happened.

A 5,000m race covers twelve and a half laps of the track. The race went off at a modest pace, and I focused on staying in a good position, knowing that someone could put in a sudden surge, and I wanted to make it possible to try to cover it. Sure enough, with nine laps to go, the Kenyan Mercy Cherono surged, stringing out the field. It was such an abrupt injection of pace, I was mindful not to cover the move too quickly, otherwise lactic acid can rapidly accumulate. The rest of the field caught back up, but the Kenyan contingent continued to stretch the pace. With six laps to go, a group of five of us had broken away – the three Kenyans Mercy Cherono, Janet Kisa and Margaret Muriuki, and Eloise Wellings, my friend from Australia, and me. Four laps to go and still it was our group of five, with only three medals available. With three laps to go, it was now or never. I hit the front. I could hear the response in the crowd: you can't imagine how it could get any louder, and then it does. The decibels carry an energy that wills you on. I tried to push on, knowing that the Kenyan athletes would be fast finishers, and the fresher they were, the quicker they'd be. My legs felt better than I thought they would, and I was actually enjoying the challenge of racing like it was a kind of game. I tried to up the pace, but I knew they were still there on my shoulder, just poised. With two laps to go I was still in the lead, trying to push harder, trying to muster all my determination, the Kenyans and Eloise still right behind me. I ran down the back straight, but with 600m to go, the four of them filed past me. I gave chase, I wasn't going to give up the fight, I wasn't finished yet.

That night of 2 August 2014, I don't know whether I consciously summoned-up an eyeballs-out effort or whether it was instinctive and my legs just did the thinking for me. I was 'in the zone'. No! This is not how it goes. I'm not done, you aren't taking this medal chance from me now. I pushed again down the home straight. At the bell, I was back in front. They're fast finishers: there was no point being behind them at the bell. I then had the thrill of being chased down again. And again I experienced the Hampden Roar. Adrenalin flowing, I tried with everything I had to keep in front of them, but yet again they responded and yet again they surged past me. Half a lap later, with only 200m to go, I was back in fourth again. I'd already battled back so many times when they'd come past me, I didn't want that to be it, to finish out of the medals. There was no way I wanted it to end that way. We went into the final bend, I tried to make up the gap that had formed. It looked and felt like the medals had gone. I was going to have to accept the expected result of a Kenyan 1–2–3. In my head I was screaming, 'Come on.' I knew I just had to give it everything so I would have no regrets.

So one last time I dug deep, pushing as hard as I could, a renewed roar from the crowd helping to fuel my efforts. Passing one of the Kenyans, Margaret Muriuki. Closing in on Janet Kisa as the line approached. I was six-hundredths of a second from reaching her. And then – I crossed the line.

I was so caught up in the scenario of nearly having caught up with her, I couldn't be sure what had happened. It was surreal. Surely the Kenyan trio had the medals? That's what everyone had been expecting. I looked at the scoreboard: Jo Pavey, ENG, third.

Bronze. I'd won a medal! A medal in a race against Kenyan runners? It was crazy. I hadn't been in a championship race for so long. I wrapped myself in the flag that someone in the crowd kindly handed me, then followed the other two around the stadium on the victory lap. I saw my mum first. She was in floods of tears, tears of joy and disbelief. Then I saw Gav with his dad and Jacob, and ran over to them. I was forty with two children – one of them a ten-month old baby: I had had no idea how realistic it was to think I could run well. I was overwhelmed by the stadium atmosphere, the result, seeing the look on Gav's face . . . The rest of the night is a blur.

I knew the next ten days were going to be madness. There would be no time to relax and try to absorb this magical experience. I had to recover and prepare for a longer race to come – the 10,000m at the European Championships in Zurich. I had so many requests for interviews and media appearances, which was flattering, but I also had to be careful to keep my mind focused on the task ahead. I needed to try both to recover and to get in some training. I needed to think about 10,000m race tactics and get ready for another championship race. It was time to get the family back to Devon, then turn around and head for Zurich. The best was still to come.

CHAPTER 25

Gold

From the unexpected – but wonderful – experience of standing on the podium in Hampden Park, enjoying the weight of a Commonwealth Games bronze medal hanging around my neck, life was quickly back to the realities of small children. First we had to get home, unpack, re-group, pack up again and move us all plus kids' paraphernalia to Zurich for the European Championships. The flight home was entertaining enough.

Transporting two children for a stay of any length requires a large amount of kit. While I had been booked onto a flight from Exeter, Gav had driven Jacob and Emily up in the car with a boot full of stuff because we wanted them to have their favourite toys, their bikes, the running buggy and so on, and we needed quite a lot of baby equipment for the holiday park in Scotland. Also, we would need a car up there to make things work. Poor Gav. A long drive with two small children can be a fraught affair and he drove the 450-odd miles from Devon to Glasgow alone with an overnight stop. We had a different plan in place for the return journey. On the way up it would not have been possible for me to take a ten-month-old baby on my lap on the flight. I was being whisked straight to the Athletes' Village where no children are allowed and Gav would not be able to pick her up until the following day when he arrived in Scotland by car. On the way back, however, it was fine for me to take Emily on the plane with me. I had team transport to the airport so Gav and I arranged that he'd drive her to the airport and I'd take her from there. I was standing around outside the terminal chatting to teammates as we loaded our bags onto trolleys, all of us laughing in relaxed post-competition mood, when I received a text from Gav saying he'd be there in a couple of minutes. I had to excuse myself: 'I've just got to go and pick up my baby from the drop-off point.' I think people thought they'd misheard. 'Pick up a bag' possibly? As I waited in the rendezvous spot, a car came to a sudden halt just ahead of me and Brendan Foster leapt out to give me a congratulatory hug, which was really nice. I collected Emily, gave Gav and Jacob a goodbye kiss and said I'd see them in Devon. Jacob was excited that he was to be allowed an iPad movie marathon all the way home.

When I rejoined my teammates wheeling a pushchair with Emily in it, they burst out laughing. I soon met up with my parents, too, who were also on the flight to Exeter. On the flight I enjoyed going straight back into 'mum mode', entertaining Emily. It was her first experience of flying but she didn't seem to worry. On arrival at Exeter Airport, we were met by my brother Matt and sister-in-law Lorna, and my nieces Olivia and Tessa who had dressed up and painted England flags on their faces. They drove us back to our house, where I found they had decorated the outside of the house with England flags. It was so sweet of them to surprise me with this celebratory home-coming.

We had a few days at home to turn ourselves around before it was time to head out to Zurich. During the championships phase of 2014, I felt extremely fortunate to be able to have my family around me. Getting the balance between total focus and extra rest when needed, yet still having family time too, helped me enormously. With ten days between the two events, it was actually a tricky period of time. If the events had been a bit closer together, then in some ways it might have been simpler. I would have needed to focus on recovery and getting my legs fresh enough to race again. But ten days meant that, on top of the business of travelling back from Glasgow and getting organised to travel out again to Zurich about a week later, I also had to fit in a couple of track sessions to stop my legs getting 'rusty' for the European Championships. And of course my local track was still closed so it was back on the road for that long round trip to Yeovil.

Again I would be travelling out to Zurich with the team, while Gav would follow the next day with the kids and, this time, my parents. There were further logistical challenges. I had a track session to do on the same day that I needed to be at the hotel near Heathrow Airport, ready to catch the flight the next morning. With the Exeter track shut, I would again need to use Yeovil – an hour away in the direction of London – so the sensible option was to do a track session en route. Gav's parents came over to look after Emily and Jacob while Gav drove me to Yeovil all packed up for the European Championships. I hopped out, did my final crucial track session, then we continued on our way to the hotel.

In the morning I met up with most of the team, who had travelled on a coach from Loughborough, only to find our flight was cancelled. We were given food and a voucher for further refreshments to spend in the airport shops, so it became a competition among us: who could buy the most food with their

£10? Our rescheduled flight was to depart from London City Airport. Luckily the coach that had brought athletes from Loughborough was still there and we all boarded it to be transported to the other airport. We sat around the small airport for hours. Despite arriving in Zurich nine hours late, I hoped to still run through my normal preparations. I was touched that physio James Davies had waited around to do my treatment and I'd asked whether it would be possible to have the ice bath I'd planned and I duly got into it just after midnight. An inflatable bath had been set up outside the hotel with just a fence partitioning it off from a section of the car park. I sat there outside in the dark in the rain. Through narrow slits in the fence I could see parked cars and hear the merriment of people returning from a good night out. I sat there hoping they couldn't see me, not for the first time thinking, 'What *am* I doing?'

By the day of my race I felt pleased with my fitness levels, but I wasn't exactly brimming with confidence, and even after that unexpected bronze in Glasgow, I certainly wasn't assuming I would be in the medals again. My concern was that I had been tapering for the 5,000m event at the Commonwealths while my rivals had been focusing on final preparations for the 10,000m at the Euros. So it was quite an unknown scenario and I missed my fellow 'OAP' Helen Clitheroe. When I looked around the call room at Zurich, I saw lots of girls in their twenties. My teammate Beth Potter was only five years old when I made my international debut in 1997.

While I wasn't assuming I'd be in reach of the medals, the race in Glasgow had definitely shown me more tactical options. Without that race, I might have been tempted to push the pace, but I had found unexpected speed at the end of the race and that gave me more confidence to sit back and race economically, knowing it might be possible for me to put in a burst at the finish. There are particular challenges in running 10,000m on the track. For a start, because of the distance, it is run as a straight final. Other events have heats and a final with eight to twelve athletes on the track, or a maximum of fifteen in the 5,000m; but in the 10,000m there seems to be no limit. They do set a qualifying time given the statistics from rankings, but if lots of people get the time you can end up with a huge field of runners to negotiate. On a road, you just get on with running your 10k, but on a track you have to weigh up the option of running on the inside lane so you don't end up running further or of running wide to keep out of trouble. You could sit on the inside lane at the back of the pack but with so many athletes in the race it can sometimes be impossible to monitor what is going on at the front. If the pace surges, or someone makes a move, you can miss the moment and be too far back to respond. In the early laps, it's important to try to be economical and not waste energy, but also to be in a position to see how the race is developing.

Beth Potter and I caught the bus from the team hotel to the stadium. It was a bit worrying when the bus got quite delayed in traffic on the way. Beth and I were both receiving texts from team management wondering where we'd got to. We tried to remain relaxed, though; getting stressed would not help the situation, and we thought we would at least get there in time to race, even if our preparation time was cut a bit short. When we finally arrived at the track, it was time to warm up – no real time to sit and settle in. For some reason during my warm-up I started to faff about which shoes I wanted to race in. I did a stride in one pair then I changed and tried another. John Bigg, an endurance coach and also the husband of the great Sally Gunnell, was amused at me being a prat about my shoes at this crucial time. It was rather ridiculous. 'Just wear those!' he said, helping me out as I seemed in no state to make a decision for myself!

Lining up at the start, I took a moment to think how lovely it was to know that both my children were in the stadium. It felt like a very special occasion. I was struck by the usual flutter of nerves but also a feeling of calmness. After the weeks and months of preparation for this race – and all the loo trips during the warm-up – I couldn't do anything now except race. I'd been at this point so many times before, channelling my nerves to use them to my advantage.

The gun went off. There were two, staggered start lines, which is normal when there are a lot of athletes in the field. After the first bend, all the runners headed for the inside lane and it became messy. The pace wasn't particularly fast. As everyone jostled for position there was a lot of unintentional pushing and barging and athletes getting spiked. Initially I tried to find space on the inside lane. However, it was really rough there, runners were getting spiked, legs bloodied. I was cutting my stride short to avoid running into the girl in front of me and that's an awkward and uneconomical way to run. As the pace was slow, I made the decision that I was better off running a bit wide to avoid getting cut up or spiked or even falling. Boxed in, I felt like I could fall any second and that would be game over. On the outside, I could simply run, rather than watching my every step.

It was a lovely, cool evening – perfect running conditions – but the first 8,000m of the race were pretty sedate. If the 5,000m race in Glasgow had gone by in a whirl, the same cannot be said of the final in Zurich. At double the distance, the 10k can seem like an eternity at the best of times. I do remember when we'd done nine laps and the lap counter said sixteen laps to go thinking, 'You must be joking. This is such a long way!' I felt reasonably comfortable, though; but it took such an immense amount of concentration to keep out of trouble, trying to avoid getting tripped or barged or boxed in. I kept in touch but decided not to get involved with what was going on right at the front until the final stages. As the closing laps approached my legs started to feel tired due to the impact of running so many laps in spikes on a hard track, not because of the distance. I remember thinking, 'Actually, my breathing is all right', and I could hear some of the athletes around me breathing hard.

With around 2,000m to go, the speed gradually picked up. At 1,400m to go, I got nearer to the front to make sure I was in a better position to cover any moves if they occurred. With three laps to go the Portuguese athletes Sara Moreira and Ana Dulce Félix injected some pace, but this was met with an immediate response from the French athlete Clémence Calvin, who took the lead and pushed the pace. With 1,000m to go, Calvin pushed harder, putting in a brave, determined effort. I was aware of not covering this sudden surge too quickly. With 800m left, I moved into third and maintained this until around 550m to go when I surged and ran past Moreira to move into second place. Just before the bell signalled the final lap, I moved into the lead.

The crowd noise rose in a crescendo as the final stages of the race begun to unfold. Spectators may have felt nervous, but I also recall a high intensity of nervous energy on that last lap. Calvin was still right behind me. Could I do it? Could I finally get a gold after all these years of trying? I didn't know, but I was in the zone, concentrating on the track in front of me. I focused on running a controlled last lap, trying to be in tune with the perceived exertion I was putting in, thinking and gauging things while I was running. I was in front, ready and waiting to put in a further boost of speed if needed. I wanted to ensure that I still had something in the tank. I focused so hard on controlling my pace, trying to prevent blowing up on the finishing straight. I didn't want to get it wrong and have athletes flying past me at the end, leaving me with nothing left to give, and legs feeling like lead weights. I needed to judge it right. At around 240m to go I surged a bit more as I felt Calvin trying to make a move. I didn't know whether she would come past me in the closing stages. But I found I still had something in reserve and I felt good. I kicked hard at 120m to go, then gritted my teeth and with about 80 metres left I put in my final kick. I didn't look around; I just ran and ran and ran. I gave it all I had, knowing that I wanted to wake up the next morning with no regrets. I gave it absolutely everything and left nothing in reserve. I focused my eyes on the finish line, willing myself towards it as if I had blinkers on. I was unaware of anything else apart from crowd noise and the finish line.

And then I crossed that line, teeth still gritted – and I'd done it. Or had I? I put my hands halfway up, not above my head. I didn't want to go mad with my celebrations in case I'd got it wrong. That would be embarrassing! But hands halfway up would be okay, as I figured I'd got a medal of some sort. I couldn't believe no one had sneaked up the inside and passed me. I couldn't believe I'd won. Surely not. Gold medals don't happen to me. I tried to look up at the scoreboard waiting for the result to flash up. But when I saw the pack of press photographers gathering in a crowd around me, I started to realise that yes, it was true, I had crossed the line first. I had won a gold medal, the very first in my long career. And I'd won it just a month shy of my forty-first birthday!

Did that truly happen to me? Yes, it did. I had the cheers of the crowd to confirm it. I was hugely moved that night by the reception I got. I'm told there was an announcement – I don't remember – that I was now the oldest ever female European Champion. I had tried for so many years to win a gold medal and to win it when I had two lovely children, both in the stadium to watch me, was so special. It was worth the wait. I ran round the back straight holding the flag on my lap of honour and finally found my family. I ran round the barriers to reach them. I hugged Gav and Jacob, and Gav handed Emily to me for a cuddle. Obviously I had not planned that moment. It was lovely to have my parents there too. I didn't think I would be doing a lap of honour as European Champion, not at my age! But it felt wonderful and the spontaneity of it was so surreal.

This was an amazing moment for me in every sense. I had enjoyed the best moment of my career at a time when I had my longed-for little family to help me savour the moment. It was such a surprise, and it was amusing in a lot of ways. However much I had always run, and tried to lead the right lifestyle for an athlete, to beat my personal bests, to run for the sheer love of it, winning this gold medal was the ultimate prize. It was something I'd presumed would never now happen. I thought the days of a gold being a possibility were long behind me. And when it finally happened, the circumstances were so far removed from what I had expected. It showed me that being happy in life, having that balance, was what led me finally to achieve something that I thought would never be possible. All the setbacks I'd fought against, the injuries I'd had to overcome, the disappointments I'd experienced – it had all been worth it.

Without this surreal experience, though, I feel I still wouldn't have looked back on my career with regret. I never wanted to mull over the 'what ifs' and the medal misses. I've been so fortunate to have had so many memorable experiences – the places I've been, the people I've met. I think that is how I would have viewed my running career even if it had ended a few years earlier, but I cannot deny that winning that gold medal was a truly satisfying experience, unmatched by anything else in my career. Celebrating with the Union flag around my shoulders, in that supportive stadium atmosphere with my parents watching, with the family I'd always dreamed of . . . Nothing can ever beat that.

It was busy at the track after the race and when I finally got back to the team hotel at 1 a.m. I sneaked back into the room, planning to sleep in my kit rather than showering because I didn't want to wake my friend and roommate, the javelin-thrower Goldie Sayers, as she still had a final coming up. Unfortunately, despite my best efforts, it didn't work, and I think I woke poor Goldie. I apologised and she was so lovely about it, saying 'Well done' and claiming she was already awake.

I only became aware of the extraordinary level of interest in my achievement the next day when I saw my picture plastered across the newspapers and was informed a host of TV crews wanted to speak to me. I was so surprised. It was so much more attention than I would have expected. Gav was taken aback by it, too. When he returned from the stadium, he and my dad were having a drink in their hotel bar while mum looked after the children. Out of the corner of their eyes, Gav and Dad saw my image on the TV screen. It was Sky News's slot reviewing the next day's newspapers. I was on the front pages for being old and a mum! I was so thrilled to be able to do a radio interview and mention my childhood coach, Tony. He could no longer see, but I knew he'd be listening to that particular programme. To think it was in his group that my distance running career started all those years ago.

We wanted the children along with Gav and my parents to see my medal ceremony, which was scheduled for the following day and the always-helpful Liz Birchall from British Athletics sorted out tickets for us all. When I met up with them all on the street outside the stadium, I had just been informed that the ceremony would probably be postponed until the next day because of weather delays to the schedule. We were told that if it was to go ahead that night, then it would be much later than the original allocated time slot. We waited and waited. I was so pleased to see Jacob and Emily again, I stayed with them and we all headed to a pub-cum-pizza-place. We couldn't make up our minds whether or not to order some food. We hummed and hawed, but still no confirmation call. Eventually we ordered food, only for me to receive the summons for the podium ceremony. Classic! We had to cancel the pizza order, which we'd only made seconds earlier, and leave for this huge moment in my career – when a gold medal was going to be placed around my neck to the sounds of the national anthem – with the words of an angry restaurateur ringing in our ears.

Standing on the top of the rostrum felt even more emotional than I thought it would. I'd heard the national anthem so many times, but it felt truly unbelievable that this time it was being played for me.

I arrived home to find that my brother Matt and his family

had this time decorated our house with British flags rather than the England flags they'd hung after the Commonwealths. It was so lovely of them – and they'd looked after our guinea pigs throughout this whole championship phase! I also received lovely cards and messages from my other brother Jon, his fiancé Deb and daughter Alisha, and all of Gav's family, our extended family and my friends. I was so grateful and overwhelmed by the goodwill and warmth, but a little shocked (and flattered) by the level of media attention. The support of the public meant so much to me, but it became a very chaotic time that I hadn't bargained for, and kept us busy juggling it around the kids. I can see it was a rather funny storyline for a forty-year-old to be confirmed as 'the best in Europe'. We tried to keep everything as normal as we could for the kids, and we weren't sure initially when BBC Breakfast asked if they could do a recorded interview with Jacob. The lovely Sally Nugent was so great with kids that we ended up having no problem in agreeing. 'What does Mummy do?' she asked him. I loved his answer: 'We go to the track. She runs about a bit, then she wears a flag and then we go home.'

During this busy time, I had to keep training too. I'd been selected to represent Europe in the Continental Cup in Morocco. When I arrived in Marrakech, I was surprised to learn that I'd been given the privilege of captaining the women's team. This was a wonderful honour, but it was such short notice, and I was expected to give a speech at the team meeting the following morning. It was hard to know what to say to athletes who were so experienced; it's much easier to address athletes who are just starting out. My main concern was to try to be encouraging but not patronising, especially as a lot of them had so many more medals than me! It went fine – and I took consolation in the fact that many of them didn't understand English, so didn't know what I was saying anyway. I finished third in the race, which I felt was a solid result, considering the busy time I'd had.

Later in the year I was honoured to receive awards that never in my wildest dreams had I ever thought I'd be considered for, including the British Sportswoman of the Year at the Sports Journalism Awards. The year ended on a truly surreal note: to finish third in the BBC Sports Personality of the Year felt like a dream! It was overwhelming, and I will always be so grateful to all the people who voted for me. When I later saw the photos of me standing on the stage next to Lewis Hamilton and Rory McIlroy, it looked as though I must have been photo-shopped on to the image!

I might have occasionally let myself dream about winning races, and even medals, but I'd never, ever envisioned the fanfare that came with that gold medal.

CHAPTER 26

At the Age of Forty

Since the 2014 season, I have often been asked why I'm still running at a high level over the age of forty with two kids in tow. At the time of writing I am forty-two and still training hard, still with goals to aim for. Technically, I've been eligible for the past eight years to compete in the World Masters Athletics series! When I chat to people, they've often said that it was actually winning gold at such a late age that made my story interesting. After the European Championships, I might as well have been renamed 'Jo Pavey-Forty'. It was as though I suddenly had a double-barrelled surname because my name was scarcely mentioned in any media coverage without my age. I enjoyed all the banter about my age, even when my GB teammates called me Granny.

So what do I put my longevity in the sport down to? It's hard to name just one factor. Obviously there is an element of luck in your genetics, plus I've always made sure I eat well. I've learnt when it's important to push myself and when my body needs a rest too. More important, I think, is having the attitude to not see age as a barrier. I try to continue as I always have, attempting to hit my times in training and focusing on goals to keep me going. I also have years of experience, as a result of which I've grown to know instinctively how to get my training mix right. But when I cast my mind back over my career, I realise that in many respects, my continuation in the sport comes down to not wanting to let go of my childhood joy of running. That passion and love for running I first discovered all those years ago is still there. Becoming a mum helped me rediscover the simple joy of running. The happiness it gave me, and the better balance in my life, has psychologically benefited my running immensely.

Since becoming a mother, my whole approach is about juggling priorities – with my kids always coming first. As soon as I was pregnant with Jacob, I decided against ever going abroad for winter training camps. I want to be a full-time, hands-on mum and there's no time now to obsess about training or to worry about trying to follow the 'perfect athlete' routine. I've found I therefore make more sensible decisions about what levels of training I can handle and how many sessions I can fit in. I do what I can, when I can, and I don't stress about straying from some idealised plan.

If it looks happy-go-lucky on the surface, I can assure you we have a well-thought-out, structured coaching plan with targets to hit, but it has built-in flexibility because my body doesn't always allow it. On a day-to-day basis, I make decisions. Can I put one foot in front of the other? And at what pace? If I go to the track, I'll ask myself whether I can run on the inside lane. No? I'll do what's realistically possible. People have the illusion that you have to be pain-free in order to compete. I know differently. For me, it's not so much about being injured or not on any one day, it's about making the right decisions to get *some* work done.

I enjoy my training and racing so much more now because I am happy. I feel life has come full circle on both a personal and a career level. I have rediscovered the simple joy of running I had as a young girl. In 2014, I was more in tune with that schoolgirl runner than at any point since I entered the elite athletics scene. I went back to the basics of pure running. There are so many ideas and gadgets out there, and some of them are great, but it's so easy to get bogged down with it all. I admit that I've been resistant to some suggestions over the years, and I've had a lot of laughter and teasing over my stubbornness – which I do express politely! When I go out of the door now, I have a sense of being reconnected to my true self, believing in simple, straightforward, sensible hard work, backed up with good nutrition and strategies for injury prevention. After having kids, it worked for me to go back to basics.

I feel fulfilled. I love being a mum who happens to run, and I love being a mum who is a professional athlete but can still come second in the primary school sports day mums' race. (Yes, a shocking halt to the winning streak I'd started at Jacob's pre-school sports day – but this was running with a tennis ball under the chin!) It's all good fun. My family unit is my training unit. I have a better balance in my approach to life. The perspective that parenthood gives me means I don't stress about the small stuff. We simplified our approach, moving back to rural Devon, stepping away from the world of high-performance centres. It was just Gav and me working together. I was back running round the same country lanes that had helped me win those junior titles, passing the same landmarks, knowing the times I should be hitting at certain points along my routes. I rediscovered that free-spirited feeling I had at the age of fourteen when everything seemed less complicated. I make sure I do my training every day, including the weekends, but what time I do it can be quite random and will depend on the children's needs.

I also owe a lot to circumstances. Had London not won the bid to host the 2012 Games, I may well have retired after Jacob's birth. I had considered winding down my track career and turning my attention to road races, but the opportunity to compete in a home Olympics was too tantalising. It was a huge deal and I wanted to be part of that. So I didn't hang up my spikes. I wanted to see if I could qualify for my fourth Olympics. Maybe it would be the swansong for my track career. And then, in finishing seventh twice behind the East Africans, I was on paper the best in Europe so – in hindsight, never along the way – my gold medal in 2014 seems a logical conclusion to a cycle that started with the goal of getting to London 2012.

Having said that, before those Olympics, Jacob was not yet at school. He was transportable and free to come wherever we went training. When Emily came along, we were managing Jacob at pre-school and Emily as a baby alongside my training with the added challenge of Emily refusing to take a bottle. With Jacob, Gav could take his share of night feeds, but I was up all night, every night, feeding Emily. She was never far from me on my runs and track sessions so I could break off and feed her. And then with the track in Exeter closed for resurfacing work, coming back from having a second baby was tough and I never would have thought that medals were a possibility. In one interview I was asked about possible scientifically proven benefits of competing after childbirth. I'm no scientist but the suggestion amuses me when I think of my own personal experience. Any supposed benefits cannot possibly compen-sate for the weeks and months you exist on a cycle of sleep deprivation – never mind the demands on your body of breastfeeding and the fact that, when you return to running (possibly after a C-section, which is classed as 'major surgery'), your starting point is a completely unconditioned body.

My approach would not work were it not *our* approach as coach and athlete, husband and wife. I find it so much more rewarding working towards goals together. And I'm very lucky that Gav has been so supportive over the years. Our circumstances give me more hours in the day to potentially 'work' in. I often do my second run of the day when the kids are in bed, and Gav always does my physio last thing at night. I don't go to the gym; instead I do exercises in the lounge often while multi-tasking or with children sitting on me. We never need to schedule a meeting or wait to have a conversation – we chat in the car, over the kitchen table or cleaning out the guinea pig hutch. We've known each other so long, and having met through athletics, the checklist of ideal work is almost intuitive between us. Gav would say that he's always had to hold me back, stop me from overdoing my training, so our family dynamic helps him in that cause! We still have plans but don't stick to them rigidly and we react to what is happening on a particular day. We know when I need to do 1,000m reps at a certain time or do 400m speed work off short recoveries. We've gained an understanding of what to do to get me in the best form we can for whatever goal we've set. I might need to do explosive speed work on a particular day, but I might also know that my body won't hold up and it's easier to be honest if your husband's your coach. Equally, the plan might be to do ten reps and Gav will tell me eight is enough.

Between us, we have our coping strategies. The main one is to remember our priorities – and that means not worrying about the housework or domestic chaos. Gav's mum kindly helps out regularly to clean the pans piled high in the utility room that are caked with food Gav has forgotten he's left on the cooker. The amount of times I've come back in from a run to find Gav on his knees, searching the recesses of the freezer for something to replace the fish fingers he's burnt . . .

One day we might have a house as immaculate as a show-home, but for now the kitchen cabinets remain unpainted and we have a messy house. We have mastered the quick tidy-up in the event of someone springing a visit on us – everything gets chucked into the understairs cupboard or thrown out of sight upstairs and Gav jokingly threatens to rugby-tackle to the ground any visitor who tries to go up the stairs. I take particular pride in the spare bed, which is piled with clean laundry that still needs ironing or putting away. Some days it's so tall it's ridiculous, but I take a sense of achievement from its height. It means I've been very busy having fun with Jacob and Emily, and training . . .

Acknowledgements

Thank you so much:

Gav, Jacob and Emily; Mum and Dad; David and Sheila Pavey; Grandad and Grandma (Alec and Stella Keightley); Grandad and Grandma (Den and Iris Davis and Auntie Babs); Gav's Grandad, John Pavey; Matt, Lorna, Olivia and Tessa; Jon, Deb, Alisha, Carisse and Jasmine; Julie, Paul, Amy, Liam and Phoebe; Alison, David, Jack and George; Alex, Janice, Sophie, Sam and Annaliese; Howard, Carol, Carolyn, Emma, Sally, Claire, Wendy, Becci, Emma, Mike, Lucy, Laura and Lesley.

John and Hazel Kimbrey; Sue and John Bloomer; Becca, Steve, Imogen, Luke and Samuel; Andy, Analie, Charlie and Lachie; Hil, Ramsay, Cher, Paul, Ciara, Lottie and James; Kathy, Andrew and Libby; Jo, Paul, Elodie and Olivia; Kirsty, Andy, Lily, Max and Iris; Denise, Niz, Zane and Ryah; Helen, Anthony, George and Samuel; Alison, Damian, Arthur, Susannah and Miriam; Julia Todd; Chi Man Woo; Ruth and Barry Godbeer; Paul Gregory; Tony White and Les Curtis; Mike Down and Chris Boxer; Mrs Sexty, Mike Gill, Eileen Mander, Penny and Dave

Gibbs, Caroline and Jim Cousins; George Eccles; Tony Proverbs (Heart of Gold winner); my friends from the village of West Hill in Devon; my team mates from the past four decades; Alan Storey; Trevor Hunt; Sarah Edworthy, Frances Jessop, Matt Phillips, Ceri Maxwell Hughes, Phil Brown and Tim Bates.

Thank you to all the team at Kingston Hospital for the care they gave to Jacob.

Please give blood: 0300 123 23 23

Massive thank you to Consultant Paediatrician Dr Rachel Howells (Royal Devon & Exeter Hospital).

British Athletics Supporters Club; thank you so much to all the athletics fans that have supported me over the years; the British medical team including Paul Dijkstra, Bruce Hamilton, Rob Chakraverty and Noel Pollock – thanks for helping me out when I was ill or injured and thanks for putting up with my very stubborn ways! Zara Ford, Pierre McCourt, Neil Black, Dean Kenneally, Gerard Hartmann, Benita de Witt, Eben Verster and Toby Smith – thank you to all the physiotherapists and osteopaths who have treated me over the years; James Davies (my physiotherapist for the 2014 European Championships); thanks to Jemma Oliver (physiotherapist Glasgow Commonwealth Games 2014); Andy Jones (Exeter University), Charlie Pedlar (St Mary's College), Raph Brandon and John Kiely; Tim Hutchings; Geoff Wightman, Kim McDonald, Ricky Simms and Marion Steininger, Jane Cowmeadow; Jonathan Marks, Emma Wade and all at MTC; Liz Birchall at British Athletics, Zara Hyde-Peters (formerly of UK Athletics), Jeni Pearce, Glenn Kearney, Adrian Harris, Lewis Jones, Marion Barnacle, Chris

Griffiths, Barry Fudge, Brian Moore; thanks to Jean Verster, Alta Verster and Olli-Pekka Kärkkäinen; photographer Mark Shearman, Frank Horwill, John Gladwin, Dave Scott, Kate Carter, Sean Ingle, Andy Dixon, Joe Mackie and Ben Pochee. Thanks to Gordon Seward, Catherine Newman and Berihu Tesfay; Exeter Harriers, my club since childhood; British Milers Club and Bristol & West AC; *Runner's World* magazine and '*AW*' (*Athletics Weekly*); David Monti, Mary Wittenberg and all at the New York Road Runners; Brendon Foster, David Hart and all at Great Run; Dave Bedford and all at the London Marathon; Steve Cram, Wendy Sly; all at Adidas UK, PowerBar and Thule; all at my home track Exeter Arena and Exeter City Council; St Mary's College, Twickenham (endurance centre and facilities), Imperial College London (facilities), The Metropolitan Police (facilities), Exe Valley Leisure Centre (facilities); Jake Hannis, South Somerset District Council and all at the Bill Whistlecroft Athletics Arena in Yeovil; Plymouth Brickfields Track; funders and sponsors both past and present, Matthew Fraser Moat and Sir Eddie Kulukundis; special mention of Dreams Come True, Exeter Leukaemia Fund, Exeter & East Devon Sports Association for the Disabled and Children's Hospice South West; thanks to those that nominated or voted for me in some of the awards that followed the 2014 season.

Finally, those countless volunteers that make sport possible. The coaches, officials and all that give up their time freely for others. Thank you so much.

List of Illustrations